I0828609

THE

HOLY COMFORTER:

HIS PERSON AND HIS WORK.

BY

JOSEPH P. THOMPSON, D. D.

NEW YORK:
ANSON D. F. RANDOLPH,
No. 770 Broadway.
1866.

NEW YORK:

E. O. JENKINS, STEREOTYPER AND PRINTER, 20 NORTH WILLIAM ST.

TO THE CONGREGATION

OF THE

Broadway Tabernacle Church,

WHOM FOR TWENTY-ONE YEARS I HAVE SERVED

IN THE GOSPEL,

AND BY WHOSE FAVOR

I AM AGAIN PERMITTED TO SEEK REST AND REFRESHMENT IN FOREIGN LANDS,

THIS

Remembrancer of my Ministry

IS INSCRIBED

BY THEIR

GRATEFUL PASTOR.

THE FATHER, of an infinite majesty;
Thine adorable, true and only SON;
Also the HOLY GHOST, the
COMFORTER.

CONTENTS.

CHAPTER I.

THE NAMES OF THE HOLY SPIRIT.

CHAPTER II.

THE HOLY SPIRIT A DIVINE PERSON.

CHAPTER III.

THE SPIRIT IN HIS RELATIONS TO THE TRUTH.

CHAPTER IV.

THE COMFORTER ALSO A REPROVER.

CHAPTER V.

SIN AGAINST THE HOLY GHOST.

CHAPTER VI.

THE SPIRIT AS LIFE.

CHAPTER VII.

THE HOLY GHOST AS DYNAMIC POWER.

CHAPTER VIII.

THE HOLY SPIRIT AS A PLENARY PRESENCE.

CHAPTER IX.

THE TEMPLE OF THE SPIRIT.

CHAPTER X.

THE TRINITY MANIFESTED BY THE SPIRIT.

CHAPTER XI.

THE TRINITY IN REDEMPTION.

THE HOLY COMFORTER.

CHAPTER I.

THE NAMES OF THE HOLY SPIRIT.

The Paraclete.

"HE shall give you another *Comforter*."[1] Jesus himself had been the comforter of his disciples, and the name *Paraclete*, by which he here designates the Holy Ghost, is applied by John to his own office of mediation between the erring disciple and the holy Father. "If any man sin, we have a *Paraclete* with the Father, Jesus Christ the righteous." The term *Advocate* by which the name *Paraclete* is rendered in the Epistle, is equally significant with the term *Com-*

[1] John xiv. 16. 1 John ii. 1.

forter in the Gospel. Neither is the exact equivalent of the original word; both alike express important phases of its meaning; and there is no one English word which will at once convey all that is consolatory in the thought of a "Comforter," and all that is encouraging in the thought of an "Advocate."

Jesus had been to his disciples a guide, a teacher, a consoler, an intercessor. They had been able to look to him continually for counsel, to lean upon him for help. As he was about to go away, he said, "I will not leave you orphans;" and he promised to make good his own place among them by sending "*another* Paraclete" who should abide with them forever. The Holy Ghost would not only console them for the absence of their Lord, but would make good to them his presence; would avert from them the sorrow, the loneliness, the helplessness of orphanage, and be to them all that Christ had been as a Paraclete. To conceive what it was for the first disciples to enjoy the personal presence of Christ is, at the same time, to realize what is the function of the Holy Ghost as the abiding Paraclete in the Church.

The etymology of this term warrants both the significations given to it in our English Bible—" Comforter " and " Advocate." If taken actively, it denotes one as calling—who calls another near for the purpose of aiding or comforting him, or calls to him by way of encouragement or cheer ; and such is the Comforter. If taken passively, it denotes one who is called near for assistance, a helper, an Advocate. Jesus both cheered his disciples by his word and was invoked by them in their need. And so the Holy Spirit is in the Church as the Caller and the Called — cheering faint and troubled hearts with his voice of peace, and ever within call of those who seek his help. The Paraclete is he who is ever at hand as helper, who stands by us in all our need ; nigh to speak to us words of counsel and of comfort, nigh to answer our call when we turn to him for aid. As one who calls, the Paraclete utters consolations or exhortations; as one who is called, he is appealed to as an advocate to maintain a cause.[1] The two thoughts are beautifully interblended in the eighth chapter of Romans; — the Spirit brings to us the comforting, animating assurance, that we are the children of God; and the "Spirit also helpeth our infirmities, and maketh intercession for us with groanings which cannot be uttered."

By the Holy Ghost, God is in the church as the Helper of yearning, sorrowing, struggling souls. He did not finally withdraw from the world when he ceased to be incarnate among men, but only changed the form of his manifestation; laid aside the flesh to reappear in the Spirit—making a manifestation not local as at the first, but universal as his church; not to wondering eyes, but to believing hearts. Thus the name "Paraclete" is the annunciation of the Divinity as Helper, as Immanuel-Jesus was the annuncia-

[1] Ebrard on 1 John ii. 1.

tion of God with us as Saviour. Man must have a God to lean upon, to trust in—whose presence he can somehow realize, whose help he can somehow feel. The Pagan represented the Deity in statue and painting, in order thus to bring him nigh to the conception of the worshipper. The Pantheist conceives of the Deity as an animating spirit in Nature, and would see him in the sky and the sea, and feel him in the pulsations of life as a very part of the universe and of man. But neither nature nor art can bring God so near to our thoughts as he comes in this manifestation of the Spirit. Never before was there such a conception of God—immeasurably grand and awful—unspeakably tender and precious—the Spirit of truth, holiness, power—abiding with human souls to help them in all their need ;—

> In us, for us, intercede,
> And, with voiceless groanings, plead
> Our unutterable need,
> Comforter Divine !

In us "Abba, Father," cry—
Earnest of our bliss on high,
Seal of immortality—
Comforter Divine.

The Spirit of Truth.

"WHEN He, the Spirit of Truth is come, he will guide you into all truth."[1] It is truth in the absolute sense which is here predicated of the Holy Spirit. Not only does he reveal truth, giving certainty to the statement of truth in the Scriptures, and definiteness to our conceptions of truth, but in him truth is vivified and personified, made real and made alive. In him truth is no longer an abstraction to be intellectually contemplated, nor a formula of doctrine to be believed; but a living power that addresses the soul through the revealed word, and also speaks within the soul itself, as with the very voice of God.

All spiritual truth, as it were, finds shape and utterance through this Holy Spirit.

[1] John xvi. 13.

The deepest things of the infinite mind are his; the secret thoughts of human hearts are his also. He can reveal what unaided reason could not discover, and can impart to the mind that spiritual discernment which looks through the veil of sense upon the spiritual realities around us, and to the spiritual glories before us. "Eye hath not seen, or ear heard, neither have entered into the heart of man, the things which God hath prepared for them that love Him. But God hath revealed them unto us by His Spirit—for the Spirit searcheth all things, yea, the deep things of God."[1]

He is the Spirit of Truth;—he cannot err, for he knoweth all things; he cannot be deceived, for he knoweth all hearts; and as Christ was the manifestation of God incarnate in love, so is the Holy Ghost the manifestation of God in the way of truth, by his holy presence and mighty power, to convince men of sin, and to renew and sanctify the heart. He is sent into the world, here

[1] 1 Cor. ii. 9, 10.

to abide as the Truth—to guide us into all truth, showing to us the things of God.

With what awe should we come to the Holy Scriptures when we remember that the Spirit of Truth is here. For God is in the Bible as in nothing else that we see or touch. The sun displays the glory of God, yet brings God no nearer than his own place in the heavens. His beams are but reflections of that glory. But God himself is in this book of truth—a living Spirit—searching our hearts when we open its pages, and speaking to us with the voice that once shook the earth. "Say not, who shall ascend into heaven, to bring Christ down from above; or who shall descend into the deep to bring up Christ again from the dead."[1] There is no further need of signs and wonders—no need of a new incarnation or resurrection—for, "The word is nigh thee, in thy mouth, and in thy heart." The Spirit of truth is here—the living God, speaking face to face, moving heart by heart. Dare we then trifle with this Word

[1] Rom x. 6, 7.

of truth? Dare we cavil at this Spirit of truth and blaspheme the Holy Ghost? Dare we neglect or despise the voice of eternal truth speaking in this Book?

But if we humbly seek to know God, he is not afar off, but nigh; not in heaven only, but on earth also; and this, not by laws or influence merely, but in the living presence of his Spirit still in the world to follow up his truth, the great argument of his love in sacrifice of Christ. More momentous than the manifestation of God in the creation, more glorious even than the incarnation —could we but discern it—is this abiding presence of God in the Church by his Spirit, to teach, call, sanctify and save!

Holy Ghost, the Infinite!
Shine upon our nature's night
With thy blessed inward light,
Comforter Divine!

Search for us the depths of God;
Bear us up the starry road,
To the light of thine abode,
Comforter Divine!

The Spirit of Grace.

THIS epithet of the Holy Spirit occurs but once in the New Testament, but in a passage of peculiar significance. In warning the Hebrews against apostacy under the new dispensation, the writer makes the crowning guilt of such apostacy consist in having "done despite unto the Spirit of grace."[1] The act here described, that of insult, clearly points to the Holy Spirit as the subject of thought; since only a living person can be susceptible to grief,—to dishonor, to insult. He is the "Spirit of grace" in that he is at once the dispenser of divine grace to the soul and the earnest of divine favor in the future. The work of regeneration and of sanctification is ascribed to him. All the graces of the Christian character — love, joy, peace, long-suffering, gentleness, goodness, faith, meekness, temperance—are the fruits of the Spirit. All the special gifts bestowed upon the early

[1] Hebrews x. 29.

Christians, and known as the *Charismata*, were the dispensation of the Spirit of grace. And the work of the Holy Spirit in the gracious recovery of the soul to communion with God is "the earnest of its inheritance, until the redemption of the purchased possession."[1] Himself the crowning gift of grace, and the author of all grace in the heart and life, he is the Spirit of grace.

We are sinful; cleanse us, Lord;
We are faint; thy strength afford;
Lost—until by thee restored,
Comforter Divine!

Like the dew, thy peace distil,
Guide, subdue our wayward will,
Things of Christ unfolding still,
Comforter Divine!

[1] Ephesians i. 14.

CHAPTER II.

THE HOLY SPIRIT A DIVINE PERSON.

Of the Personal Pronoun.

THE descriptive titles of the Holy Spirit clearly imply a Person of whom the various functions of Helper, Teacher, Sanctifier are predicated. As Jesus was a person, so "another Paraclete" who should come in his stead to abide with the disciples, to teach them all truth, to comfort them in sorrow, to succor them in need, must fairly be assumed to possess the properties of personality — consciousness, understanding, will, affections; and these all are attributed to the Holy Spirit. It was not simply a divine agency, influence, attribute or power, concerning which the promise of "coming" and "abiding" was made, but a distinct personality.

The term "spirit," indeed, is not conclusive upon this point, since this is often used to denote simply an influence, power, or energy, proceeding from a person or thing, and not of necessity the personality of an intelligent being. When we speak of the spirit of patriotism, the spirit of loyalty, the martial spirit, as animating a nation, we attach no thought of personality to the word. And, again, when we speak of a man as actuated by a certain spirit, as showing a spirit of benevolence, or self-denial, or public spirit, the word describes the temper, disposition, or action of a person, and not the person himself as one possessing such and such attributes. Hence, some have argued, that in the Scriptures the term Holy Spirit describes an influence or energy proceeding from God, and not a distinct person.

It must be admitted that in the Old Testament the phrase "Spirit of God" or

"Spirit of the Lord" may sometimes signify the will or energy of the divine being under certain forms of activity. The declaration that "the Spirit of God moved upon the face of the waters" might be taken simply as an announcement of the Spiritual Essence of the Creator. Only by spiritual power was creation possible. And though we read in the Hebrew Scriptures that "the Spirit of God" came upon Balaam, Saul and others and prompted their prophetic utterances, were there nothing more explicit in the Bible touching the personality of the Holy Spirit, we might understand by such phraseology simply a divine energy or influence acting in the manner described. But it is impossible thus to explain the language of the New Testament touching the Holy Spirit. For the New Testament speaks of the Spirit in terms only appropriate to a person—applying to him the personal pronouns, and all the attributes and actions of a distinct personal existence.

But this, it may be said, was in the oriental style of personification, as, for example, in the book of Proverbs, *Wisdom* is personified—described by personal pronouns, and as speaking and acting as a person. She is represented as dwelling with God from eternity, taking part in the creation, coming forth to guide men to virtue and life. But this is obviously a *poetic* representation—as when Milton says,

> "Hail, holy *Light!* *Thee* I revisit now!"

apostrophizing the Light as if it were a living, intelligent substance.

Such personification is frequent in poetry. But there is no trace of poetry in the last discourse of Jesus to his disciples. In the solemn and tender hour that intervened between the institution of the Supper and his going forth to the agony in Gethsemane, when he would fain comfort and strengthen the hearts of his friends so burdened with sadness and fear, Jesus did not speak to them in parables. There was no vague generalization concerning the love of God, no metaphorical representation of the coming of divine influence upon their souls, but the definite promise of another Paraclete to take his place and abide with them; a PRESENCE, which though not corporeal and visible like his own should be real and felt; another coming of God into the world, so wondrous in its nature, so glorious in its effects, that Jesus must needs withdraw his corporeal presence, that this spiritual presence might be had in his stead. "I will pray the Father, and he shall give you another Comforter, that he may abide with you forever, even the Spirit of Truth; the Comforter, which is the Holy Ghost, whom the Father will send in my name, he shall teach you all things."

The Scriptures apply to the Holy Spirit the personal pronouns and personal properties in a way that cannot be reconciled with the idea that the Spirit is only an influence or energy proceeding from God, but lacking consciousness and personality. To speak thus of an unconscious influence,

[1] John xiv. 16, 17 and 26.

would be an extravagance in language for which there is no warrant even in the highly wrought poetry of the East. In the words just quoted, there cannot be a question that Christ and the Father were spoken of as persons. Whatever view may be held concerning Christ—whether he is regarded as man merely, or the created head of the universe, or as God—all sects and schools agree that he had a personality distinct from the Father.

In the promise "I will pray the Father, and he shall give you another Comforter," we clearly recognize a distinction of persons;—the *I* who prays, is a person; the Father who gives or sends, is also a person. How then can we regard the Comforter who is sent, as a mere unconscious influence, when the same personal pronoun is applied to the Spirit: "HE shall teach you all things."[1] By what rule of interpretation, by what example anywhere in human lan-

[1] John xiv. 26. *τὸ πνεῦμα τὸ ἅγιον ἐκεῖνος ὑμᾶς διδάξει πάντα.*

guage, could we justify such a violent transition from the personal actors in the beginning of the sentence to an impersonal agent at its close, while yet the personal pronoun is applied as freely to this agent the Spirit, as to the Father and the Son? True, the term Spirit—*Pneuma*, is neuter; but this was the term by which the human soul as an intelligence was distinguished from the body; and God is himself a Pneuma.[1] And the same pronoun is applied alike to the Father, to the Son, and to the Holy Spirit. "The Comforter, the Holy Ghost, whom the Father will send in my name, he [not *it*, but] *he* shall teach you all things."[2] "If I go not away, the Comforter will not come unto you; but if I depart I will send [not *it*, but] *him* unto you; and when *he* [not *it*] is come, he will reprove the world of sin. . . . When *he* [not *it*] the Spirit of Truth is come, he will guide you into all truth. . . . . . HE shall glorify ME."[3]

[1] John iv. 24. [2] John xiv. 26. [3] John xvi. 7, 8, 13, 14.

Can this repeated, purposed and significant use of the personal pronoun with respect to the Holy Spirit, denote anything less than his distinct personality? To warrant such language as Jesus used in describing his coming, must he not possess consciousness, understanding, will, affections, in a manner as distinctly personal as were these properties in Christ himself?

Of Personal Offices and Acts.

"IT is impossible to prove the Father to be a Person, or the Son to be a Person, any other way than we may prove the Holy Ghost to be so. For He to whom all personal properties, attributes, adjuncts, and operations are ascribed and to whom nothing is ascribed but what properly belongs to a Person, he is a Person; and so are we taught to believe him to be. Thus we know the Father to be a Person, and the Son also. . . . . . But there is no personal property belonging to the Divine Nature that is not equally ascribed to the Holy Ghost."[1] In addition to the unqualified use of the personal pronoun with reference to the Holy Spirit, the Scriptures ascribe to the Spirit such acts and relations as are possible only to a Person, and which could not with any propriety of speech be ascribed to an unconscious influence. "The Holy Ghost *spake* by the mouth of David;[2] . . . . . and by Esaias the prophet."[3] On the day of Pentecost the Spirit *gave utterance* to the apostles through unknown tongues.[4] Jesus had distinctly promised that the Holy Ghost should be the teacher and prompter of the disciples in the propagation and defence of his Gospel: "Whatsoever shall be given you in that hour, that speak ye; for it is not ye that speak, but the Holy Ghost."[5] "The churches walked in the fear of the Lord and in the comfort of the Holy Ghost."[6]

[1] Dr. John Owen, on the Holy Spirit; chapter iii.
[2] Acts i. 16. [3] Acts xxviii. 25. [4] Acts ii. 4.
[5] Mark xiii. 11. [6] Acts ix. 31.

The Spirit speaks of himself as a Person having authority in the church. "The Holy Ghost said, separate [unto, or for] *me* Barnabas and Paul, for the work whereunto I have *called* them."[1] He directed that they be set apart for the missionary work, and he *sent* them forth to the Gentiles. Then, in the course of their tour they were *forbidden* by the Holy Ghost to go to this or that place,[2] and in all their steps were under his direct personal control. It was the Holy Ghost who made the elders at Ephesus overseers of the flock of God.[3] It is the Holy Spirit who teaches, guides, enlightens, comforts, sanctifies believers ; it is he by whom both Jews and Gentiles have access to the Father ; it is he who helps our infirmities in prayer and "maketh intercession for the saints according to the will of God;"[4] it is he who dwells in the renewed heart as in a temple, and who strengthens us "with might in the inner man."[5] But such acts

[1] Acts xiii. 2. [2] Acts xvi. 6. [3] Acts xx. 28.
[4] Rom viii. 27. [5] Eph. iii. 16.

and operations as these can be affirmed only of a *person*, not of a mere influence. The Holy Spirit is described as having supreme knowledge and as imparting wisdom to others. He is described as distributing his gifts according to his own will. He has affections also, and can be grieved, offended, resisted, as a person.

The fearful warning of Christ to such as are guilty of blasphemy against the Holy Ghost, and the saying of Peter to Ananias, "Satan hath filled thy heart to lie unto the Holy Ghost"[1] are decisive of the personality of the Spirit. Can men commit blasphemy against an influence or an attribute, which has no consciousness? Can one lie to a thing, an emanation, an energy, which has no life or intelligence?

"If a wise and honest man should come and tell you, that in a certain country where he has been, there is an excellent governor, who wisely discharges the duties of his office; who hears causes, discerns right, dis-

[1] Acts v. 3.

tributes justice, relieves the poor, and comforts the distressed; would you not believe that he intended by this description, a righteous, wise, diligent, intelligent person? . . . Could you imagine him to mean that the *sun* or the *wind*, by their benign influences, rendered the country fruitful and temperate, and disposed the inhabitants to mutual kindness and benignity? and that the governor was a mere *figure* of speech? It is exactly thus in the case before us. The Scripture tells us, that the Holy Ghost governs the church; appoints overseers of it; discerns and judges all things; comforts the faint; strengthens the weak; is grieved and provoked by sin; and that in these and in many other affairs, he works, orders and disposes all things, according to the counsel of his own will. Can any man credit this testimony and conceive otherwise of the Spirit, than as a holy, wise, intelligent Person? Can such expressions refer to a quality, an effect or influence of the power of God, who doeth all these things *figura-*

tively; that he has a *will* figuratively; and *understanding* figuratively; is *sinned against* figuratively and so of all that is said of Him?

"It is true that some things peculiar to persons are sometimes ascribed to things; as Charity is said to hope, to believe, to bear; the Scripture is said to see, and foresee, to speak and to judge. The heavens and the earth are said to hear; and the fields to sing and clap their hands. But these ascriptions are only *occasional,* and a plain description of the things themselves is given us in other places. But as to the Spirit of God, the constant uniform expressions concerning him are such as declare him to be a *person,* endowed with all personal properties."[1]

[1] Dr. John Owen On the Spirit, chap. iii.

The Spirit a Divine Personality.

IT is conceded even by those who deny the Trinity in the godhead that the Holy Spirit is divine, since they regard the Spirit as only an influence or emanation from God. But we have seen that the Scriptures clearly teach the personality of the Holy Spirit, and they no less clearly affirm the divinity of this personality. What is the distinction in the godhead set forth by the terms Father, Son and Holy Ghost, we may not be able to state with philosophical precision; only we can affirm with John Howe, that "as it cannot be less than is sufficient to sustain distinct predicates and attributions; so it cannot be so great as to intrench upon the unity of the godhead; which limits on the one hand and the other, God hath himself plainly set us."[1] It is enough for the present argument that the Scriptures teach that the Holy Spirit, who is distinctly a per-

[1] Howe's Calm Discourse of the Trinity. Works Bohn's edition, p. 137.

son, is in his nature divine. Every attribute of divinity is ascribed to the Holy Spirit as fully as to the Father.

The Spirit is omniscient—for he "searcheth all things even the deep things of God"[1] —he knows the mind of God in its inmost depths as truly as a man knows his own thoughts through consciousness. The Spirit is omnipresent—for at the same instant he can witness his presence in the hearts of believers who are separated by the earth's diameter—making intercession for you, as you kneel in your ceiled closet, and at the same time for the converted Hottentot who steals away among the bushes that he may cry "Abba, Father." The Spirit is omnipotent; he inspired the minds of the apostles, revealing the things of the invisible world and things to come; he gave miraculous powers to the early disciples; for all these things, miracles, gifts of healing, prophecy, tongues, "worketh that one and the selfsame Spirit, dividing to every man sever-

[1] 1 Cor. ii. 10, 11.

ally *as he will.*"[1] All supernatural gifts are his, and in their dispensation he is a sovereign, doing his own pleasure. Can He who knows all human hearts and rules the realm of supernatural powers, be less than God? The Spirit has infinite wisdom. He knows all truth; he is the truth; he guides men into truth—showing to them the things of God.[2] The Spirit is declared to be eternal,[3] which as an attribute of existence can be applied only to God; and in a word, every attribute and work that belongs to the Deity alone, is ascribed without qualification to the Holy Ghost.

Moreover, he is expressly called God. Peter said to Ananias, "Why hath Satan filled thy heart to lie to the Holy Ghost?—thou hast not lied unto men but unto *God.*"[4] And in the formula of baptism and the apostolic benediction, the Holy Ghost is by name associated with Christ and the Father. This indicates both his personality and his

[1] 1 Cor. xii. 11. [2] John xiv. 26 and xvi. 13, 14.
[3] Hebrews ix. 14. [4] Acts v. 3, 4.

divinity. "Go teach all nations," was the Lord's command, "baptizing them in the name of the Father, and of the Son, and of the Holy Ghost."[1]

We baptize in the name of a person, not of an influence ;—and would any one less than God be associated with his name in this solemn act of consecration? We speak indeed, of being baptized with the spirit of patriotism *i. e.*, consecrated to the service of the country. The Israelites were baptized to Moses, *i. e.*, they covenanted under his leadership to obey the word he had received from God; but they were not baptized in the *name* of Moses and of Jehovah. It would shock all piety and reverence, if one should baptize in the name of the Father and of the Son, and of Paul, or of Moses, or of the angel Gabriel; or in the name of the Father and the Son and the Bible, or the truth, or of a divine influence. In this most solemn transaction, the public consecration of a human person to God by baptism, we

[1] Matt. xxviii. 19.

can associate with the high and sacred name of Father only the names of *persons* who are with himself in Being, Power and Glory. And when the apostle gives forth the benediction—" The grace of the Lord Jesus Christ, and the love of God, and the communion of the Holy Ghost be with you all,"—the laws of language and the sense of fitness demand that we regard the Holy Spirit as divine.

CHAPTER III.

THE SPIRIT IN HIS RELATIONS TO THE TRUTH.

The Spirit in the Written Word.

WE have seen that the Holy Ghost is called the Spirit of Truth, and the teacher of truth. The Scriptures were indited through an influence from the Holy Spirit upon the minds of their several writers ;—" No prophecy of the Scripture is of any private interpretation"—it was not merely the prophet's own conception or exposition of the will of God—" for the prophecy came not in old time by the will of man; but holy men of God spake as they were moved—incited and borne along—by the Holy Ghost."[1] And the gospel of the

[1] 2 Peter i. 20, 21.

New Testament was preached by the apostles "with the Holy Ghost sent down from heaven;"[1]—"which things we speak, not in the words which man's wisdom teacheth, but which the Holy Ghost teacheth;" for "eye hath not seen, nor ear heard, neither have entered in the heart of man, the things which God hath prepared for them that love him"—mere human speculation had not attained to these sublime discoveries—"but God hath revealed them unto us by his Spirit."[2]

Our knowledge of the Holy Spirit in his direct personal relations to the truth is derived primarily from the Bible; yet in the constitution of the human mind and its conscious spiritual wants, we find a preparation for—an adaptation to—this very manifestation of God; and in the process and effects of regeneration and sanctification, we find certain phenomena or experiences which this doctrine of the Holy Spirit as the Revealer, the Illuminator and the Applier of Truth,

[1] 1 Peter i. 12. [2] 1 Cor. ii. 9, 10, 13.

fully explains, and which no philosophy that leaves out of view the Spirit acting in and by the truth, can adequately explain. When we say then, that the doctrine of the Holy Spirit as a divine personality manifesting his power in human consciousness by the truth, is purely a doctrine of revelation, we do not mean that this is contrary to reason, that it is unsupported by facts in the world of mind, or even that it is unintelligible ;—but only that the first distinct idea upon the subject is given us in the Bible, not formed by us from our own reflections upon facts of observation and experience. This idea received from the Scriptures, explains facts already within our knowledge and experience, and those facts in turn confirm the doctrine.

If you arrive after dark in a strange valley, you may be puzzled in the night to decide whether the sound you hear is the rain, or the wind, or a waterfall, and may hold a disputation concerning it without reaching a conclusion—but when in the morning sun you look out and see the stream pouring down the hill-side, you say at once, " Ah, this is what I heard in the night;"—so when you see a man shaken in his soul as by a mighty wind, and suddenly changing his whole course of life, and you " hear the sound thereof, but cannot tell whence it cometh and whither it goeth," but in the clear light of God's word you read, " So is every one that is born *of the Spirit*,"[1] you say now " this explains it all ; for though I cannot yet distinguish *how* it was, I see clearly *whose* work it is." This is " the testimony of God, in demonstration of the Spirit, and of power ; that your faith should not stand in the wisdom of men, but in the power of God."[2]

In considering the function of the Holy Spirit as the revealer of truth, we should carefully define the sphere of human philosophy upon such a subject. Plainly there can be no *a priori* reasoning about it ; that is, we are not competent to say, before com-

[1] John iii. 8. [2] 1 Cor. ii. 1–5.

ing to the Scriptures, whether God exists in one person or in three—or whether in the sphere of mind he acts directly as a person, or only by laws and influences, such as he is supposed to employ in the world of matter.

From the study of natural phenomena we deduce the law of gravitation, the law of attraction, the law of magnetic influence;—we do not need to go to the Bible to discover these, and the Bible says nothing about these. But we cannot argue that, because in the world of matter, God works largely by fixed laws and established influences or forces, therefore in the world of mind he must act only by fixed laws, and never by a direct personal power. In the nature of the case, our knowledge of God is so limited, that with respect to the mode of his existence and his operations, we can not affirm beforehand what God is or is not, or what he can or cannot be, or do. Upon such a point, holding our philosophy in suspense, because it has no data to work upon, we must first, as wise men, endeavor to learn what God has revealed concerning himself; and with the facts thus ascertained from his testimony, we can reason about them and apply them to what we know of the human mind and its operations. That is to say, our philosophy in this matter must not attempt to make the facts, nor to determine upon merely natural grounds what *ought to be* the facts touching the existence and the operations of God as a Spirit; but our philosophy must reason upon the facts as given to us in the word of God. We can get the facts from no other source.

But while the personality and the work of the Holy Spirit lie beyond the discovery of unaided reason, yet when made known by revelation from God, far from being contrary to reason, they rationally explain and corroborate other facts already known. Hence the fact of such a manifestation of God as is given in the Holy Spirit working in and by the truth, is not unreasonable nor unintelligible, and therefore not incredible as a *fact*, though its philosophy may still lie beyond our grasp. We believe upon sufficient evidence the fact as we here find it to be revealed; and it is not necessary that we should explain or attempt to explain the manner of the Spirit's working through the truth, in order rationally and heartily to believe that he does so work. That must be a bold man, indeed—a most audacious man—who would say that he understands the constitution of the human mind and the nature of God so thoroughly, that he knows it to be impossible for the divine Spirit to act directly upon our minds; and he must be a weak man indeed—most foolishly weak—who would say that he will not believe what the Bible teaches concerning the power of the Holy Spirit in the truth, until he can see just how, when, and where that Spirit acts. Our wisdom is, to lay aside speculation till we come at the facts; and to seek for these by a careful and honest study of the Word of God, where, in the nature of the case, the facts can alone be found.

Inspiration of the Apostles.

THE Apostles claimed that they spoke and wrote under the dictation or the direction of the Holy Spirit. I use these two words, dictation and direction, to mark the distinction between a special revelation by the Holy Spirit, and his guidance in interpreting and expounding truth. The apostles had both the ordinary and extraordinary manifestations of the Spirit. The Saviour promised them that the Comforter should teach them all things; should guide them into all truth: "He shall receive of mine, and shall shew it unto you;" "he will shew you things to come."[1] These promises cannot mean less than that the Holy Spirit by direct communication with their minds, would make clear to them what then seemed so obscure touching the character and mission of Christ; that the Holy Spirit would interpret to them in a new light the teachings and the death of their Lord; would recall

[1] John xvi. 13, 14.

his words in their true meaning, would guide them to a true understanding of what was enigmatical or mysterious, and would reveal to them the future things of his kingdom ;—in a word, the promise included both the *revelation* of truth to their minds by supernatural teaching, and the *inspiration* of their minds for the clear perception and statement of truth and for prophetic utterances. The Book of Acts and the letters of the apostles give convincing proof that this promise was fulfilled. The Comforter did make clear to their apprehension the divine mission of Christ for the work of redemption ; he did guide them into the truth so that they had no further doubt concerning the person of Christ or the design of his death ; he did strengthen them by the conviction of truth, and with moral courage, so that they spake the Word of God with boldness ; he did comfort them with his presence, coming to their help in every emergency, so that the very men who had skulked away when their Lord was led to the judgment hall, now openly confronted priests and rulers with the testimony of Jesus, and "daily in the temple, and in every house, ceased not to teach and preach Jesus Christ," refusing to be silenced, and "rejoicing that they were counted worthy to suffer shame for his name."[1] And when we pass on to the epistles, we find a wonderful clearness, depth and power of reasoning, and an earnestness of conviction upon spiritual subjects, and especially in unfolding the redemptive work of Christ, and the life of the soul in him, from the pens of Peter and John who were at the first confounded at his death, and the pen of Paul who at first despised the name of Jesus and persecuted his followers.

This change can be accounted for by none of the ordinary or natural transitions of human thought or feeling. Men intelligently and ardently devoted to a principle or a leader, have rallied with a new vigor from seeming defeat, and have drawn fresh

[1] Acts v. 41, 42.

life and energy from the graves of martyrs. The fall of a Winthrop, a Lyon, a Baker at the beginning of the war, was but the rising of many who should wrest victory from disaster. Men who had misjudged or calumniated a patriot or reformer while living, have afterwards done honor to his memory and given their own lives to his cause. But these first Christian disciples were men who, while their leader was living, though they loved him with all devotion, failed to comprehend him or his teaching, and who imagined that his death was as much a surrendry on his part as a triumph of his enemies ;—who after his death, did not rally round a principle, a system, a cause to which they were before committed, but renounced alike the prejudices and the expectations they had clung to while their leader was with them, and took up a view of himself, his character, and his mission, utterly opposite to their fond hopes of the Messiah in his life-time, and opposite as well to the apparent facts of the case—as wide as possible from any natural and merely human schemes and calculations ;—and having embraced this view, they staked their all upon it, and with no possibility of earthly advantage, but at the daily risk of life they proclaimed their new-found doctrine of salvation for sinners through faith in a divine Redeemer. How shall we explain this fact?—how reconcile the views and conduct of the apostles in the book of Acts, with their views and conduct as recorded by the evangelists, except by their own testimony ;—" We are his witnesses of these things ; and so is also the Holy Ghost, whom God hath given to them that obey him."[1]

Any other theory of this change is as wide of the mark as that of the mockers who said: "These men are full of new wine." We first see these men weak, ignorant, timid as children, afraid to be forsaken by their Lord, yet all forsaking him and fleeing every man to his own place.

[1] Acts v. 32.

We hear, however, the promise of the master "I will send the Comforter; he shall teach you all things;" and again, after his resurrection "ye shall receive the power of the Holy Ghost coming upon you and ye shall be witnesses unto me;"[1] and presently we hear them teaching in every tongue the name and doctrine of Jesus; we see them with personal boldness and with most effective power witnessing for Christ; and the word at their lips convincing and converting the multitude. Facts such as these, which no philosophy of human nature could explain, are made clear and credible by the single statement that the Holy Spirit, as promised by Christ, had manifested Himself in the truth and in their hearts by the truth. Thenceforth the preaching of the apostles was throughout "a ministration of the Spirit." It is impossible upon any other theory to account for the establishing of the Christian Church amid storms of obloquy and persecution.

[1] Acts i. 10.

Revelation and Inspiration.

THIS ministration of the truth by the Spirit was two-fold—by dictation and by direction. Sometimes the apostles received truth by express revelation—the Holy Spirit dictating or suggesting to their minds what lay beyond the power of human discovery. This they declared, and confirmed the declaration by signs and wonders of the Holy Ghost; and this the very subject-matter of their teachings upon divine and eternal things requires us to believe.

"Eye hath not seen, nor ear heard, neither have entered into the heart of man, the things which God hath prepared for them that love him;" the doctrines of redemption and of the sanctification and glorification of believers in Christ, could never have been invented by the mind of man; no philosopher hath penetrated so deeply the counsels of divine wisdom; no poet hath soared so high upon wings of divine love; but

"God hath *revealed* them unto us by his Spirit;—for we have received not the Spirit of the world;" the doctrine we teach is not the sensuous philosophy that measures human happiness by the gratification of present desire, nor the more refined intellectualism that still rises not above the human in its conceptions and aims; but "we have received the Spirit which is from God; that we might know the things that are freely given to us of God"—the treasures of wisdom and happiness revealed by Him—"which things also we speak, not in the words which man's wisdom teacheth, but which the Holy Ghost teacheth."[1] From time to time, as Christian doctrine required to be unfolded, or as believers were prepared for higher disclosures of the work of God in redemption, special revelations were made to the apostles by the Holy Spirit. Thus the relation of Gentiles to the Gospel kingdom was communicated to Peter by express revelation, when he was called to

[1] 1 Cor. ii. 8–14.

visit Cornelius. And Paul speaks of his knowledge in the mystery of Christ, as that which is "revealed unto the holy apostles and prophets by the Spirit."

But this revelation of unknown and otherwise unattainable truth was by no means the sole agency of the Spirit in the apostolic ministry.

Inspiration, that teaching and guidance of the Holy Spirit which would authenticate their preaching as of divine authority, was not limited to the special revelation by the Spirit of things unknown. This influence present in their minds, giving clearness, definiteness, force to their conceptions and utterances, bringing to remembrance words of Christ in their true meaning, showing the things of Christ under new aspects and relations, all this was that divine guiding into truth, which was the promise of the Father and the legacy of Christ in the gift of the Holy Ghost.

The Truth a Life-Power.

NOT only did the Holy Spirit inspire the truth as uttered and recorded by prophets, evangelists and apostles, but he abides in the truth as a life-power to the souls of men. One who is acquainted with Dante only through an English version fails to perceive much of that depth and beauty of meaning which for six centuries have so delighted the cultivated mind of Italy, and have given to the author of the Divine Comedy a foremost place among the great poets of the world. The marvelous illustrations of the poet from the pencil of Doré may quicken such a reader's perception of Dante's meaning by embodying it in more tangible forms, and by exhibiting the power of the poet over the imagination of the artist. If now the reader should acquire the Italian language, and read the poem under the guidance of a competent and sympathetic Italian scholar, his soul would be penetrated with a power and beauty more subtle than the pictures of Doré can convey. Something of the spirit of the poet would infuse itself into passages before unintelligible.

But if, in such a frame, the reader could hear the voice of Dante himself, and through his intonation and expression catch his every shade of thought, the whole work would glow with a new life. Even so after we have many times read some passage of the Scriptures with but a vague and sluggish sense of its meaning, and by the help of commentators and teachers have tried to realize what it is that has stirred the genius of Raphael and Leonardo da Vinci, of Milton and of Dante himself, there will come in some favored hour a glow of light and life upon the printed page that seems to transform it into a present voice of God. To explain this, would be to explain the mystery of the divine ; to deny this is to deny the possibility of the divine.

The Spirit in Preaching.

THE doctrine of the abiding presence of the Holy Spirit in the Word of God has its correlative in the doctrine of his personal influence upon the human mind through its excitation under the truth. It is because of this that the preaching of the Gospel may be expected to produce effects which would not result from a merely human wisdom and eloquence exercised upon the same themes. The New Testament ascribes the regeneration of the soul and its sanctification in the higher life to the direct action of the Holy Spirit through the truth. The renewed soul is "born of the Spirit;"[1] the true baptism is "the washing of regeneration and renewing of the Holy Ghost;"[2] believers are chosen "through sanctification of the Spirit unto obedience and sprinkling of the blood of Christ;"[3] they "have purified their souls in obeying the truth through the Spirit."[4] And so whenever the truth of God

[1] John iii. 5.
[2] Titus iii. 5.
[3] 1 Pet. i. 2.
[4] 1 Peter i. 22.

comes effectively into contact with the mind of man—this is by virtue of the Holy Spirit who is Truth, who convinces the world of sin, who teacheth us all things.

All true Scriptural preaching proceeds upon this basis. The Christian ministry was inaugurated by the Holy Spirit, and it can only fulfil its office in the world, when in the mind of the preacher and in its effect upon the hearer, it is a "demonstration" or a setting-forth of the truth convincingly as proceeding from the Spirit and power of God. To us remains an interest in that great and precious legacy of Christ—the promise of the Spirit of truth to abide with his disciples and guide them into all truth. As Tauler, one of the most effective preachers of the middle ages, interprets the promise: "The Holy Ghost will not teach us all things, so that we shall know whether there will be a good harvest and vintage, whether bread will be dear or cheap, whether the present war will come to an end soon; but he will teach us all things which we can need for a perfect life; and for a knowledge of the hidden truth of God, of the bondage of nature, of the deceitfulness of the world, and of the cunning of evil spirits. *Thus*, when the Holy Ghost comes to us he teaches us all truth."

The preaching of the Gospel is not human argumentation and persuasion upon certain theses of theology and ethics, but a medium of communication between the divine *Spirit of truth* and the souls of men. The argument is good for expounding the truth and making it plain; the persuasion is good for drawing men to receive and obey the truth; but the virtue of preaching lies not in excellency of speech or of wisdom—not in the rhetoric or the logic of it—but in the manifestation of the truth to every man's conscience, and this comes to pass efficiently, not through persuasive words of man's wisdom, but by the demonstration of the Spirit wielding in the moral world the power of God.

This doctrine of the influence of the Holy

Spirit through the truth points to the true dignity, worth and power of the pulpit. It troubles me not that with the change of times, the advance of popular education, the growth of the press as a power, the increase of private and public libraries and of the means of knowledge in the community, the ministry as a learned profession is less conspicuous and perhaps less influential than in the early days of New England. It troubles me not that the opinions of a minister have less authority than when he was almost the oracle of the town, and that there is less deference for his person and office than when the congregation rose as he entered the meeting-house, and stood uncovered as he passed out of the porch, and when Dr. Bellamy could break in upon a festival which he deemed improper, and order the members of his parish to their homes. I have no fear that the Christian ministry is losing ground because such things have passed away. Nor do I apprehend that the pulpit is void of power if its weekly utterances do not find large audience of the people—if not every preacher is a Whitfield, a Summerfield or a Spurgeon. I remember that slender, scholarly preacher of Northampton, in voice and manner delicate as a woman, reading his notes almost without gesture, but setting forth the truth with such clearness and precision, such gravity and solemnity, and withal such inward fervor, that his voice was sometimes drowned in the sobs and groanings of an assembly smitten by the great power of God. I remember too, that Nettleton, so wise in winning souls, preferred to talk in the lecture-room or the school-house, and was little at home in the higher efforts of the pulpit; but his speech was in demonstration of the Spirit and of power. The dignity, the worth, the power of the ministry pertain not to the gifts or accomplishments of the man, nor to the sanctity of his office—whatever the theory or the mode of investiture—but to its relation to the work of the Holy Ghost in the hearts of men by the ministration of the truth. We are "laborers together with God"—there is the dignity;—"let a man so account of us, as of the ministers of Christ and stewards of the mystery of God."[1] We are "ambassadors for Christ"—there is the function and its worth: "Our Gospel came not unto you in word only, but also in power, and in the Holy Ghost. And we have this treasure in earthen vessels, that the excellency of the power may be of God and not of us."[2] All natural gifts, all human attainments should be consecrated to this high and sacred work; all study, and care, and culture should be bestowed upon the performance of its duties; but all are too mean to give it dignity, too poor to give it worth, too weak to give it power; the eloquence of a Chrysostom, the learning of an Owen, the logic of an Edwards, the fervor of a Baxter combined in one, could add nothing of dignity or power to the preaching of the Gospel; for in this high matter of proclaiming divine truth for human salvation,

[1] 1 Cor. iv. 1. [2] 1 Thess. i. 5, and 2 Cor. iv. 7.

"we are not sufficient of ourselves to think anything as of ourselves; but our sufficiency is of God, who also hath made us able ministers of the New Testament."[1] How shall not then the "ministration of the Spirit," transcending all human wisdom and persuasion, "be rather glorious?"[2]

The true function of preaching is performed in proportion as the divine Spirit of truth is thereby brought into contact with the minds of men to reform, sanctify and control them. That body of truth in which the Holy Spirit is specially manifested is given us in the Gospel. The Bible not only was inspired by the Holy Spirit, but is inspired by that Spirit who dwells within the letter as a quickening power; and the office of the ministry is, by studying to know the mind of the Spirit, so clearly, directly, earnestly to bring out the truth, that in the consciences of men it shall be demonstrated as of the Spirit of God. The increase of church and pulpit power is to be sought by pastors and people in this direction.

[1] 1 Cor. iii. 5. 6. [2] 2 Cor. iii. 8.

Pyrotechnics not Power.

WE cannot hope to increase the power of the pulpit by modifying the doctrines of the Gospel, or by substituting something else for the Gospel as the subject-matter of pulpit discourse.

We may thus increase the popularity of the pulpit, as a rostrum for stump oratory, or a desk for philosophical disquisition. We may make the pulpit a higher sort of Lyceum, good in its way as an educating power in literature, philosophy, economics, politics, taste, manners, morals, ethics ;—but preaching as an institution of Christ for the largest and highest welfare of mankind, can be true to its function only by studiously and scrupulously proclaiming the truth of the Gospel, in reliance upon the Spirit of God. Bring all possible mental power and training to bear upon the investigation of truth ; bring all possible eloquence and culture to bear in the presentation of truth ;—yet must we never lose sight of the fact that the preaching is appointed to *unfold the truth* and nothing else, and that its efficacy will be in proportion as by the Spirit of God it brings home that truth to the hearts and lives of men.

We could not increase the power of a steam-engine by turning off the steam from the piston-chamber to blow through a calliope; we should make more noise and attract more attention, but should not add to the motive-power. Nor could we increase that power by taking the steam-engine in pieces and making a hundred sewing-machines of its materials. We should get more clatter, more apparent animation, more motion in a small way, but gain no motive *power*. The only way to increase the power of a steam-engine is to enlarge its capacity for generating steam.

We cannot increase the power of the pulpit by modifying the Gospel or substituting something else for the Gospel; we must bring the preaching into a larger, freer, fuller union with the Spirit of truth. You could not have subdued the rebels by setting up Edge's fire-works in sight of Richmond and letting off brilliant pieces on the Union, Liberty and the Constitution. We conquered by using the powder in rifled cannon and well-made bombs. No pulpit pyrotechnics will subdue the rebellion of the heart. For this we need the whole armor of God, and especially "the sword of the Spirit which is the Word of God."

Preaching not Infallible.

BUT while insisting that the function of preaching is to unfold the truth of the Gospel according to the mind and by the power of the Holy Spirit, we must guard against ascribing to the utterances of the pulpit, however sound and true, the infallibility that belongs only to the inspired word. The power of the Spirit pertains not to the man, nor to *his* words as if suggested by inspiration, but to the truth which he brings forth from the Word of

God. It is the very essence of fanaticism that one imagines himself inspired with divine wisdom above his fellows, and then imperiously and vehemently insists that men shall accept his opinions, under penalty of excommunication here, if not damnation hereafter. Popish dogmatism, infallibility and intolerance lose even the pretence of antiquity and veneration in a Protestant pulpit, and sink into a pitiable egotism. The doctrine of the Spirit's influence in preaching, warrants no claim of inspiration and authority in the preacher; his office is so to interpret the truth, as to manifest *that* to every man's conscience in the sight of God.

Preaching to be Practical.

BUT it is no less a mistake to assume that, since preaching is to be the unfolding of Gospel truth by the power of the Holy Spirit, therefore it can have to do only with the spiritual acts and exercises of the soul, and not with the morals and the manners of the life of society. Just because preaching is not the setting forth of human advice and opinion upon secular affairs or the details of life, but the endeavor to bring the Spirit of truth into the heart to reform and to sanctify it, therefore should the preaching carry that truth into every thought and feeling of the man, and every act and interest of the life. See how the Spirit himself deals with human life in his application of the truth. He begins with the individual heart, bidding that become regenerate and holy; he applies truth to the family, bidding husbands love their wives, and wives reverence their husbands, and children obey their parents in the Lord; forbidding all jealousy, impurity, contention, disorder in the household; he carries truth into the church-relation, requiring mutual love and helpfulness, forbidding all partizanship, clanship and caste; all domineering of rich over poor, of strong over weak; he applies truth in society, teaching men how to use money, and women how to adorn themselves; forbidding frivolity and revelry as offensive to himself, —"be not drunk with wine, but be filled with the Spirit;" forbidding the lust of the flesh, the lust of the eye, the pride of life; he carries the truth into business — requiring things honest in the sight of God and man, and forbidding all lying and fraud; he carries truth into social relations and institutions, requiring just and equal wages, brotherly kindness, good-will to all, and thus making it impossible that a Christian should treat a fellow-man as a chattel, or that a Church seeking his presence should harbor such a crime; he applies truth to civil government, teaching us to support government as a divine ordinance, and yet in a conflict of human and divine law to "obey God rather than man;" and thus everything, eating, drinking, dress, wages, business, marriage, the family, conversation, company, politics — the whole circle and work of human life—comes legitimately within the sphere of the pulpit, not for human dogmatism but for the unfolding of the mind of the Spirit through the Word of truth. He is the truest minister who most faithfully and successfully brings home the truth of God to the every day life, and causes all human words and works to be tested by the searching Spirit of Truth.

CHAPTER IV.

THE COMFORTER ALSO A REPROVER.

His Coming to the World.

THE coming of the Paraclete was not intended solely for the comfort and edification of the Church of Christ. Only to the disciples of Jesus would the Spirit come as the Comforter; only to them would he come as an inspiring power; only with them would he abide, witnessing in their hearts by all gracious affections and fruits, that they were born of God—and taking up their broken cries of penitence and their yearnings after holiness, with his own sympathetic "groanings," pour these with "unutterable" intercession into the bosom of the Father.

But beside this mission to the hearts of

the disciples, the Spirit would come to the world at large in the demonstration of his power. The world had rejected Christ. Blinded to the purity and innocency of his life, and the righteousness which he wrought out and exemplified for men, the world branded him as an imposter. The world in the persons of the Jewish Sanhedrim and the Roman Governor, sat in judgment upon Jesus, condemned him as a blasphemer—" making himself the Son of God;"[1] as a seditious pretender—" saying that he himself was Christ a King;"[2] and the world cast him out to be crucified. But he who yielded so meekly to all this insult and injury, who suffered himself to be " led as a lamb to the slaughter," who, before his accusers and tormenters was dumb " as a sheep before the shearers," hath sent the living, personal, almighty Spirit of God, to convict the world of its guilty unbelief in rejecting the Redeemer, to vindicate the personal righteousness of Jesus in that God

[1] John xix. 7. [2] Luke xxiii. 2.

had put to his testimony the seal of the resurrection; to set forth also his propitiatory righteousness, in that he who "was delivered for our offences, was raised again for our justification;"[1] and above all, to convince the world that the cross of Christ was a tribunal also; that the prince of this world who had thought to defeat the mission of Christ by the ignominy of his death, was himself there judged and condemned; his power broken; his victims enfranchised; that the cross stands as the great test of character, and the judge of the moral state of man; and that in this spiritual condemnation of sin and Satan through the cross, there was foretokened that higher judgment when "he that loved us and washed us from our sins in his own blood," shall "come with clouds," and "every eye shall see him, and they also which pierced him."[2] When He, the Paraclete, the Spirit of truth is come, he will convict the world of sin because they believe not on me;

[1] Rom. iv. 25. [2] Rev. i. 7.

he will convince the world of my righteousness, because though despised and rejected of men, I go to the presence and glory of the Father; he will strike through the world a terror of the judgment to come, because by me the prince of this world, the very head and front of iniquity, the incarnate spirit of evil, is judged and condemned.[1]

Such is the sublime mission of the Spirit in and upon the world at large. To the church his office is mainly that of instruction and consolation; to the world his office is primarily that of conviction, with a view to repentance and regeneration. In the ear of the believer, the Spirit whispers of acceptance, adoption, peace, joy, fellowship with God; in the ear of the sinner, the Spirit cries the warning of sin proved upon the conscience; of righteousness enthroned in Christ; of judgment even now going forth in condemnation, because of unbelief. The

[1] John xvi. 8–12. See also Hare's "Mission of the Comforter."

Spirit is in the world for Reproof and Conviction; "Reprove" our English Bible has it; "convince" it is in the margin;—a better reading, though neither is quite full or strong enough. One may be reproved or rebuked without being brought to a conviction of his fault; "reproof" or "accusation" may be unjust, or if deserved may be ineffectual; but, the word used by Jesus,[1] "implies not merely the charge, but the truth of the charge, and the manifestation of the truth; nay, more than this, very often the acknowledgment if not outward, yet inward, of the truth of the charge on the side of the party accused; it being the glorious prerogative of the truth in its highest operation not merely to assert itself, and to silence the adversary, but to silence him by *convincing him* of his error or wrong."[2]

Thus did the Spirit convince the world upon the day of Pentecost, when there came

[1] ἐλέγξει. John xvi. 8.

[2] Archbishop Trench, Synonyms of the New Testament. ἐλέγχω.

upon the disciples the power of the Holy Ghost, and to the very multitude who had rejected and crucified Christ, Peter declared his divine mission as their Messiah, his perfect righteousness and regal supremacy, and their guilt in refusing him. "Jesus of Nazareth, a man approved of God, as ye yourselves also know, him ye have taken, and by wicked hands have crucified and slain ; Him God hath raised up."[1]

Thus did the Holy Ghost bring home to them, sin, righteousness, judgment, till they were pricked in their heart and cried "Men and Brethren what shall we do?"[2]

The Work of Conviction.

THE conviction of sin in the human soul is none the less the work of the Holy Spirit to-day than when with tongues of fire he accused the murderers of Christ. The commonness and universality of sin ob-

[1] Acts ii. 22, 23, 24. 32. [2] Acts ii. 27.

struct or impair the conviction of personal sinfulness. In the mephitic atmosphere of a depraved world, conscience itself becomes sluggish and is well-nigh paralyzed. Averse to self-inspection, partial in judging themselves, familiar with sin by habit, accustomed to superficial standards of character in society, men would never of their own accord look upon sin as it appears in the sight of God. The very sin which, under the Gospel, is the specific ground of condemnation — the unbelieving rejection of Christ—is by men regarded as an indifferent matter of opinion. Therefore has the Holy Ghost come into the world to convince men of sin.

By what subtle laws or what special action the Holy Spirit produces conviction, it is not given us to know. But the fact that he is in the world to convince it of sin is a satisfactory explanation of the frequent phenomena of involuntary conviction. Conviction may be the sequence of a voluntary introspection of the motives of conduct,

But though a man take pains to avoid reflection, and to ward off the reproofs of conscience, conviction will often come in spite of him and overwhelm the conscience with its power. For conviction is light; and it is not possible to shut out all light from the soul. Conviction is feeling, springing up spontaneously from mysterious depths; and it is not possible to seal up conscience so that it will no more be agitated. Conviction is memory recalling past misdeeds, bringing them up at unawares to confront us in their guiltiness, stripped of all the excuses and disguises that covered them at the time.

Conviction may be forced upon the mind by a thinking that it does not invite, and yet cannot repress. And when through so many avenues, the conviction of sin is pressed home upon the mind without its seeking or consent, we may well believe that this is the work of the Holy Spirit. Though men may "always resist the Holy Ghost" by refusing to turn from their sins, his power to *convince* them of sin is irresistible. He knows avenues to the soul that preachers cannot reach, and yet that sinners cannot bar. One may keep himself away from sermons and Christian appeals, or he may rebut argument and ward off reproof; yet while he fancies himself safe in his sins, some stroke of Providence from without, or some unaccountable uneasiness within, will bring him under an agony of conviction. He may bolt his door against all human access, and then lie down to toss upon his pillow with the torments of remorse. "I remembered God and was troubled. Thou holdest mine eyes waking. I am so troubled that I cannot speak."[1]

As with those rebel ports which were fortified against every approach from the landward side, yet lay open toward the sea, the sinner may entrench himself in his position, and fortifying his mind against all human approaches, may defiantly run up the flag of rebellion; but while he is thus

[1] Psalm lxxvii. 4.

secure upon the landward side, the great ocean of truth rolls around him, and God is Sovereign there. And when the divine forces come sailing in, and deliver their blows of rebuke and conviction upon the inmost citadel of conscience, every blow shaking down defences, exploding errors, kindling within and about him the fires of retribution, his boasted arguments are dismounted; he dare not trust himself upon his own battlements, he cannot sight his resistance against such a power; the battle is within his fortifications; and though he may remain an unrepentant rebel, he finds his "refuge of lies" a prison and a hell.

His Reproof Infallible and Irresistible.

I REPEAT, then, that while conversion can be effected only with the free action of the human will, the conviction of sin by the Holy Spirit is irresistible. This arises from the fact that the Spirit has direct access to the mind, can penetrate through all habits and disguises, and strike at the very centre of the soul.

Your watch is out of time and you try by moving the regulator now forward, now backward, and changing the hands every day at XII. and every evening at IX., to keep it in harmony with the city clocks. But all your experiments fail. The hands upon the face, the dial of the regulator, do not reach the seat of the evil; nor can any such inspection as you are able to make, detect the real cause of the irregularity. But the instant your watch-maker fastens upon it his microscopic lens he detects the dust that clogs the wheels, or the congealed oil about the pivots, or the spring strained till its wonted elasticity is gone, or coiled irregularly and therefore playing with uneven beat. He puts his pencil or his forceps upon the very seat of the irregularity and points out the defect. You might have taken the watch apart and have discovered nothing; but from the symptoms of the disorder and his knowledge of the interior structure he knows just where to look for the cause. It may be that the derangement which you supposed to be slight has communicated itself to the whole mechanism; so that instead of regulating, your watch requires cleaning; instead of a new crystal and key or a new dial plate, you need a new main-spring—perhaps a new motion throughout.

Now the Spirit, as the author of the mind, goes direct to the seat of the evil that is in the mind. He knows what causes the derangement. If the dust and soil of this world have clogged the sensibilities and aspirations of the soul for good, he at once detects it. If fleshly lusts pervert the will and draw the soul from God, the Holy Spirit can detect and expose this. The mental analysis of a Hume or a Hamilton, might no more discover the cause of the aberration than your analysis of your watch would reveal its defects. But the author of the mind can go behind all forms and barriers, all appearances and shields, to the very inmost springs of life and action; he can search out the evil there, and cause us to see and own it also. Not only can he infallibly detect the evil, but he can irresistibly expose it to our view. The watchmaker causing you to look through his lens while he should point out the interior of your watch, might enable you to comprehend the nature of the difficulty. But the author of your mind, when he searches out its hidden evil, can compel you to see it; can so quicken the eyes of conscience which you had sealed, that you *must* see yourself as you are in his eyes. He can bring upon you the sense of God's immediate presence, and of your accountability to him as your judge. Did the sinner stand face to face with God he would have no cloak for his sins. Did he feel that all-seeing, all-searching eye fastened upon his inmost soul, he would need no voice of God to charge him with his guilt and pollution. To the guilty soul, the thought of God as a pure, holy, and just Sovereign, is attended with a secret dread of meeting him in judgment. The contrast of his own character with the character of God is that of darkness with light, of impurity with holiness;—and such holiness and light as might blast him by its very shining. Therefore he shuns the thought of God. But the Holy Spirit can bring the eye of God upon his soul so that he shall feel it there; can give him glimpses of him who is invisible, the law-giver, the judge, which shall cause him to cry out, "Behold, I am vile. Now mine eye seeth THEE, wherefore I abhor myself and repent in dust and ashes."[1] "*He shall convince the world of sin.*"

[1] Job xl. 4, and xlii. 5, 6.

CHAPTER V.

SIN AGAINST THE HOLY GHOST.

Of Grieving and Resisting the Holy Spirit.

IN considering the operations of the Holy Spirit in the human soul, we should never lose sight of the fact that he has to do with that which is spiritual in its essence, and voluntary and free in its powers and modes of action. It is because of this that the Scriptures warn men, with a dread emphasis of repetition, against resisting, grieving, and quenching the Spirit. The personal influence of the Holy Spirit upon the mind to bring it to repentance may be resisted to the last by a stubborn or reckless will. The power of the Spirit to convince men of sin, we have seen, indeed, to be irresistible. But conviction is not conversion; the consciousness of guilt is not repentance. If it were so, there would be no ground for the distinction between repentance and remorse; and well nigh all mankind would be converted, since at some time they are convicted of sin. Conviction rests in the understanding and the conscience; but conversion involves distinctly an act of the will. The will may not be able to ward off conviction from the understanding and the conscience, but the will can and often does resist the end of conviction, which is conversion. Hence the power of the Holy Spirit, however irresistible in the way of conviction upon the understanding and the conscience, may be resisted by the will at the essential point of turning from sin to holiness. The distinction lies in the nature and sphere of the will, and in the nature of sin and holiness as voluntary states of the soul.

The change which the Bible, under various figures, describes as a new birth, a new creation, a resurrection from the dead, is a radical change of moral character, whose seat is in the will and the affections. It cannot take place but with the free consent of the will; for it lies in the choice of God and holiness in place of self and sin; it consists in renouncing sin and the world as objects of affection, and transferring the heart's best affections to God, its supreme love and devotion to his cause. This must be voluntary to have any worth; it must be voluntary or it cannot be at all. The physical terms under which it is symbolized, birth, creation, resurrection, and the like, would be mutually contradictory if taken literally, yet these are none too strong to describe the thoroughness of the change. But such a change cannot be mechanical. The Holy Spirit may come to the mind with overwhelming force of conviction; may silence the arguments and cavils of unbelief, may fill the understanding with a blaze of light, may kindle the conscience to a fiery glow of rebuke, may even touch the emotions and affections so as to awaken yearnings toward a higher life, aspirations, desires to be freed from the yoke of sin, to be reconciled to God, may seek to draw the will back to its forsaken allegiance—but just then and there, where the man must decide for himself, he may do "despite to the Spirit of grace."[1]

The Unpardonable Sin.

THE Scriptures teach that there is a sin which "shall not be forgiven unto men."[2] What is that sin that holds this dread preeminence of guilt and condemnation? Idolatry? That breach of the second commandment, so directly offensive to God, was forgiven again and again to apostate but repenting Israel. Adultery? David bewailing his guilt with a broken and contrite heart, was purged as with hyssop from that crime. Murder? Saul of Tarsus with his hands yet dripping with the blood of the

[1] Heb. x. 29. [2] Matt. xii. 31.

saints and his tongue fuming out blasphemy against the name of Jesus, was forgiven and made a chosen vessel to bear that name to the Gentiles. Lying and profaneness? Peter denied his Lord with oaths and curses, yet Jesus appeared to Peter after his resurrection and commissioned him to feed his sheep and his lambs.

This unpardonable sin is nothing gross to outward appearance, perhaps not even startling to the mind itself. It is not to be sought for in the category of the vilest crimes; it does not stamp the sinner in human eyes as with the brand of Cain. It lies directly between the soul and God; and no outward sign may indicate to the world how or when it is committed. And yet the awful verdict has gone forth from the lips of the Son of God, "All manner of sin and blasphemy shall be forgiven unto men; but the blasphemy against the Holy Ghost shall not be forgiven unto men."[1]

Jesus himself was despised and rejected,

[1] Matt. xii. 31.

mocked, scourged, crucified as an impostor, yet on the cross he prayed for the forgiveness of his murderers. But those lips of gentleness and love, breathing forgiveness for every injury against himself, uttered also the warning of this unpardonable sin: "Whosoever speaketh a word against the Son of Man, it shall be forgiven him: but whosoever speaketh against the Holy Ghost, it shall not be forgiven him, neither in this world, neither in the world to come."[1]

The beloved disciple, who reflected so much of the gentleness of his Lord, and who sets forth so fully the efficacy of the blood of Christ to cleanse from sin, and the efficacy of prayer through the Redeemer's intercession, says expressly, "If any man see his brother sin a sin which is not unto death, he shall ask, and God shall give him life for them that sin not unto death." This phraseology alone would suggest that there is a limit somewhere to forgiveness—a limit somewhere to the power of intercessory

[1] Matt. xii. 32.

prayer. And then the apostle adds, with a point and emphasis that may well strike the soul with awe, "There is a sin unto death; I do not say that he shall pray for it."[1]

What that sin is, we are taught in such passages as these: "He that shall blaspheme against the Holy Ghost hath never forgiveness; but is in danger of eternal damnation;"[2] or to speak more strictly, is judicially subjected to a condemnation, which, as the sin will never be remitted, must be eternal. This is the sore and hopeless punishment of one who hath "trodden under foot the Son of God and hath counted the blood of the covenant wherewith he was sanctified an unholy thing, and hath done despite to the Spirit of Grace."[3] The unpardonable sin is the knowing, wilful, persistent, contemptuous, malignant spurning of divine truth and grace, as manifested to the soul by the convincing and illuminating power of the Holy Ghost.

[1] 1 John v. 16. [2] Mark iii. 29.
[3] Hebrews x. 29.

The Warning of Christ.

WHEN Jesus by the Spirit of God had cast out devils, the Scribes and Pharisees said: "He hath Beelzebub, and by the prince of the devils casteth he out devils."[1] Now this name Beelzebub was a name of contempt for one of the vilest of the heathen deities. No more gross or insulting epithet could have been applied to Jesus, than this which represented him as acting under the influence of the most unclean of spirits. Yet he could forgive the insult, the derision offered to himself; but he warns them of that blasphemy against the Holy Ghost that shall not be forgiven. No personal resentment moves his reply—no vindication of his own dignity and honor from the foul aspersion—but an awful sense of the sin against the Holy Ghost.

The Pharisees saw with their own eyes the deaf and dumb made to speak and hear,

[1] Matt.

by the casting out of the devil that possessed him. The evidence of their senses, and their training in the Jewish faith, alike taught them that this was a direct act of divine power. They knew the fact; they could not deny it. But as selfish, grasping rulers and managers, they could not bear to see the people turning away from their authority to follow Jesus; and therefore they derided him, and sought to fasten upon him a contemptuous and loathsome epithet. They went contrary to evidence, to reason, to conviction, to their own religious faith; they did this wilfully and spitefully for selfish ends. Jesus ascribes this miracle in the sphere of evil spirits to a direct manifestation of God as the Spirit of holiness and power; and therefore warns them lest their derision of himself be also blasphemy against the Holy Ghost: for *that* is the unpardonable sin.

It would seem that this sin is singled out for a condemnation so extreme and final, because, in the power of the Holy Spirit acting directly upon our spiritual nature, God himself comes nearer to the human mind than in any outward manifestation of his attributes, in works of creation, providence and redemption. And therefore, the scornful rejection of the evidences of the Spirit, the resistance of truth and conviction brought home by *his* power, is the highest affront to the majesty, the goodness, the glory of God in his own person ;—for it is God in person and not any work, messenger or agent of God, that is offended in the Holy Spirit.

And again, by his coming in the Holy Ghost, God makes the highest manifestation that the nature of mind and the action of spiritual powers can admit of, for the conviction, illumination and sanctification of the soul : and therefore, when this is spurned, God's utmost grace is thrust away, and judgment must have its course. And hence to do despite to the Spirit of Grace is to thrust away all hope and all mercy, and to despise God in the personal operation of his mind upon ours, to bring us to himself. In the nature of the case, by the laws of spiritual action and re-action, this act must consign the heart to irrevocable obduracy.

CHAPTER VI.

THE SPIRIT AS LIFE.

Seen in the Hebrew Prophets.

"DID the Hebrew Prophets speak as they were moved by the Holy Ghost? Did they so speak as no men but they and the apostles, have ever spoken or written? We should seek a reply to this question in the answer that must be given to another question. Is there a life divine—is there a life of the soul toward God? Is there a communion of the finite spirit with the INFINITE, on terms of intimate correspondence in which the deepest and the most powerful affections of human nature are drawn forth toward and centred upon the perfections of the INFINITE BEING? If there be—and there is—a life of the soul toward God—a life not mystical, not vague and abstractive —then we find our reply to the *included* question concerning the Hebrew Prophetic Scriptures ; for it is in these, and it is nowhere else—no, not to the extent of a line, a fragment—it is within this range that the Spiritual Life is embodied, and is expanded and is uttered in a distinct and articulate manner. It is within the compass of the Hebrew Poetic and Prophetic Scriptures that all moods and occasions—all trials and exercises—all griefs and perplexities—all triumphs and all consolations—all joys, hopes and exultations—all motives of patience, and all animated expectations of the future, find their element and their warrant also. In a word, if there be a life of the soul toward God, and if this life be real, as toward God—then are the Hebrew writers true men of God ;—then is it certain that they were instructed and empowered—each of them in his time—to set it forth, for the use of all men, to the end of the world."[1]

[1] Isaac Taylor, Spirit of Hebrew Poetry, chap xvi.

The Soul in Spiritual Death.

THE life of the soul in God which is portrayed in the Scriptures, is produced subjectively by the Holy Spirit who awakens the soul to a new life-principle and power. Sin and holiness are contrasted as death and life. The sinning soul is under a law of spiritual death—already dead, in fact, in trespasses and sins. And when we consider what the soul of man is, with what faculties and powers it is endowed, and of what attainments and enjoyments it is capable; — not merely a sentient creature with most exquisite susceptibilities and tastes; not merely an animal organization of wondrous delicacy and perfection, and with the highest variety and combination of powers and adaptations for use and for pleasure; but a rational creature, capable of knowing its relations to its Maker and to the universe—capable of comprehending the reason and propriety of things, and the principles and motives that should govern its actions ;—a voluntary being, having the power of choice ; not under mere natural law nor the control of habit, nor the direction of instinct, nor subject to coercion like "dumb-driven cattle ;" but capable of knowing right from wrong, good from evil, of choosing between them, choosing freely and without dictation, and of fixing its will and its affections upon such objects as it may choose ; a being having a consciousness of its own thoughts, motives and actions, "self-knowing," as Milton describes it, so that it need not act in anything from blind impulse—but conscious of its own personality, of its powers, of its obligations, conscious of its thoughts, motives, feelings, affections ; a being endowed also with a conscience—quick to pronounce upon the morality of actions, to urge the right and forbid the wrong ; a being capable of indefinite progression in knowledge and love, and of the very perfection of virtue—in one word a being capable of knowing and loving God, and of becoming like God in holiness and in joy;—when we thus consider the nature and capacities of the human soul, we see that the true end of such a being is moral perfection, and that its development in intellect, heart and will should always be in the line of conformity to the character of God, and the requirements of his law.

When the soul fails of this development, when its thoughts, its motives, its aims, its activities are not God-ward, nor in the direction of its truest, noblest end, then to all intents it is even as dead. The grandest functions of its being are unperformed—the one great object of its creation not only unattained but unattempted. In the low region of sentient existence, as a mere creature related to sensible objects of earth and time, or as a creature of intellect and affections, concentrating these upon the narrow sphere of self and its related interests, of this life and its arrangements, the man may seem all alive in activity and enjoyment. But with respect to that sphere of moral life, purity and joy, for which every power and faculty of the soul was adapted and designed by its maker, such a one gives no sign of life, performs no true function of his being. He makes no development of his rational and voluntary powers on the high plane of virtue. He does not seek to know God; he does not aim to love God; he does not strive to be like God; he sees no beauty in holiness; he hears no voices of truth and goodness speaking from heaven to his inmost soul; so far as God's honor and glory, God's will and end in his existence are concerned, he is as one dead.

Every adaptation he has, indeed, for that original end and glory of his creation; every means within reach for its accomplishment—the latent power and capacity for living unto this high end—but all his faculties so blinded and bound by sin, that he has no spirit within him toward such a life. Only when the principle of holiness enters into union with the natural powers and faculties of the soul, vivifying and controlling these, only when thus pervaded and animated by a loving obedience to God, does any soul begin to live.

Life not Self-originated.

WHAT now shall raise the soul from such a death as this?—what shall send through this spiritual organism—bound by sense and sin, as Lazarus was bound hand and foot with grave-clothes—the quickening pulses of a new and higher life, awakening it to holy, loving thoughts of God, to noble purposes of duty, to self-purification, to prayerful vigilance against sin, to a delight in the law of God, and aspirations toward moral perfection? What shall restore this fallen creature to God's original design in the creation of a soul in his own image?

All experience teaches that it will never come to this true and exalted life simply of its own motion. True, it is endowed with every capacity for such a life;—capable of discerning truth; capable of discriminating right from wrong; capable of knowing God; capable of appreciating virtue; capable of approving holiness; and capable of loving him whose character is the highest expression of holiness. With respect to capacity for its proper life, as an intelligent being the soul has need of nothing.

Nor can we find any defect of natural constitution with respect to voluntary powers. The power of choice in all moral acts pertains to the nature of man as a moral being. If this freedom did not exist, there could be no responsibility: since to compel the will by a coercive power from without would be to destroy it as a will. It belongs to the very nature of the will that it is not capable of compulsion, but, within the sphere of moral conduct, has entire freedom of choice and of action.

But while this is true of man's adaptation or capacity for the higher life, and his latent natural ability to pursue that life, it is none the less true that the soul does not, and will not, enter upon a life of holiness simply of its own motion. It may make fitful and painful efforts in that direction ; it may try to arouse itself to a life of holy obedience ; but it will not enter upon and sustain such a life of itself. As with Paul, the inward man, the awakened conscience may approve the law of God ; but there is "another law in the members warring against the law of the mind," sinful lusts against reason, against judgment, against conscience ; bringing the man "into captivity to the law of sin which is in his members."[1] He is like one who, in attempting his own life, or by overindulgence in opiates, has taken so much laudanum that he has brought upon his faculties the stupor of death. If he shall be revived, it must be by the reaction of his own vital powers against the stupefying potion ; but this vital action within must be stimulated by most vigorous appliances from without. The effort is not to put into him, as by miracle, some new power of life to resist the

[1] Rom vii. 23.

invasion of death, but to call into action the vital forces that are still within the man, but are sinking into a fatal lethargy. So in this attempted suicide of the soul, or this overindulgence of the sensual nature, which has brought upon the seat of life in the soul the benumbing grip of death, there is the capacity for life, and the latent power of a higher, nobler activity; but this will not arouse itself, and as in some horrid nightmare, the very will lies impotent before the stupendous peril.

Truth alone will not give Life.

NOR will life be imparted to the soul merely by truth, though it be the revealed truth of God. The truth may startle, awaken, convict, terrify, but of itself it brings no life. Nay, truth alone may be but the agent of death. For to a mind made suddenly conscious of its guilt and its need of holiness, and stirred to some effort in that direction, the naked truth concerning God as a righteous sovereign and judge — the hater of iniquity—the truth embodied in the form of law requiring perfect obedience in holy living, may but smite the soul with a deeper dread, by bringing it under sentence of condemnation. "The law worketh wrath,"[1] and so the soul that is already dead in trespasses and sins, is twice dead by the sentence of death upon it from the law of God. "The letter killeth;"[2] mere naked truth, truth in the form of precept, by showing what is required for God's favor, kills out hope in the soul just awaking from its sins, and brings upon it the killing sentence of the law and the judge.

"If there had been a law which could have given life, verily righteousness should have been by the law."[3] But there is no life-giving power in naked law. The law requires holiness, does not impart it. The law condemns the want of righteousness—does not supply that lack. To a being who

[1] Rom. iv. 15. [2] 2 Cor. iii. 6. [3] Gal. iii. 21.

has not sinned, the law adopted into the soul may be the principle and power of an endless life ; but once sin has entered the soul, the law follows only to rebuke and condemn ; and thus "the commandment which was ordained to life, is found to be unto death."[1]

The Divine Quickening.

IT is obvious then that the spiritual resurrection of the soul must be effected by a power extraneous to itself ; a power which acts not mechanically, nor spasmodically, nor yet miraculously, but in harmony with the constitution of the soul and the laws of its moral agency and responsibility. It is a degradation of the term law, to restrict it to phenomenal sequences in the physical world. And it is a degradation both of the nature of God and the nature of the soul to suppose that nothing can come to

[1] Rom. vii. 10.

pass between God and the soul, save within the plane either of physical causation or of an absolute necessity.

A theistic writer who denies the possibility of the miraculous within the sphere of physical laws, and who therefore rejects the supernatural claims of the Bible, has nevertheless recognized, upon metaphysical grounds, the intercommunion of the Divine Spirit with the human soul ;—that, "there is a world of realities behind the world of appearances which alone our senses perceive, and that the fixed chain of necessary sequence, which binds all things in the world of sense, cannot bind the supersensible world, whereof (as well as of the lower) man is an inhabitant by right of his two-fold nature. . . . . . God is himself a Supersensible Being ; and so also, in his highest nature, is man—Creator and creature meet then in that world where the chain of physical laws has never been extended." [1]

[1] Religious Duty, by Frances Power Cobbe, p. 183.

No philosophy is competent to affirm that supernatural powers cannot operate directly upon the human spirit, and this in harmony with its own modes of thought, feeling and action. Neither the powers nor the laws of the spiritual world are sufficiently understood to warrant such an affirmation. But on the contrary the moral renovation of the human soul, changing all its aims, tastes and desires with respect to spiritual objects, is a phenomenon which is fully explained by the teaching of the New Testament concerning the quickening, energizing power of the Holy Spirit acting upon the mind through the truth.

The Scriptures always ascribe to the Holy Ghost the authorship of spiritual life from its beginning in regeneration, through the whole growth of sanctification, until the perfection of life shall be attained through a spiritual and glorified body united with a perfected soul. Jesus in his discourse with Nicodemus declared, that to enter into the Kingdom of God, every one must be "born of the Spirit;"[1] and we are saved according to the mercy of God, by "the washing of regeneration, and renewing of the Holy Ghost;"[2] "we are washed, we are sanctified, we are justified in the name of the Lord Jesus, and by the Spirit of our God."[3] We are chosen to salvation, "through sanctification of the Spirit and belief of the truth"[4] — "elect according to the foreknowledge of God the Father, through sanctification of the Spirit, unto obedience and sprinkling of the blood of Jesus Christ."[5] We pray in the Spirit, we walk in the Spirit, we are an habitation of God through the Spirit; all the graces and virtues of the Christian life are the fruits of the Spirit; and the promise to all believers is, "If the Spirit of him that raised up Jesus from the dead dwell in you, he that raised up Christ from the dead shall also quicken your mortal bodies by his Spirit that dwelleth in you."[6] Thus the whole process of

[1] John iii. 8. [2] Titus iii. 5. [3] 1 Cor. vi. 11.
[4] 2 Thess. ii. 13 [5] 1 Peter i. 2. [6] Romans viii. 11.

bringing man from death to life, beginning in the quickening of the soul to that spiritual life which emancipates it from the bondage of the flesh, and culminating in the union of a spiritual and glorified body with a sanctified and perfected soul—this whole wondrous work of life is the direct work of the Holy Spirit.

Methods of the Spirit's Operation.

THE mode of the Spirit's operation our Lord has likened to the invisible wind. But as science takes observations of meteorological phenomena though their laws may yet be inscrutable, so it is reasonable and scientific to accept the facts of the Spirit's operation in the world of mind, though the methods of his work are not discoverable by reason nor revealed in the Scriptures. Two general statements at least, are warranted :

(1.) The Spirit imparts life to the soul by bringing home to it with convincing, persuasive, efficient, saving power, the way of life revealed in the Gospel. Even that amazing expression of the love of God which is given in the sacrifice of Christ to take away our sins, stands as a dead letter upon the page of history, until the Spirit of God makes it alive to us and makes our hearts alive to it.

Hawthorne represents the sculptor as standing pensively before his own completed work, and saying: "The inevitable period has come—for I have found it inevitable in regard to all my works—when I look at what I fancied to be a statue, lacking only breath to make it live, and find it a mere lump of senseless stone, into which I have not really succeeded in moulding the spiritual part of my idea."[1] And the despairing sculptor is ready to destroy his work with his own mallet. Such a feeling is not the disappointment of a novice at his imperfect skill; rather it increases with the growth of the ideal in the mind of the artist; and there

[1] The Marble Faun.

is a tradition that Michael Angelo himself on completing one of his grandest works—the statue of Moses—dashed his chisel at it in a frenzy of despair because it would not speak. The human soul made perfect in all powers of organization and of action, educated by the most careful masters, and chiselled as it were to the most artistic point of culture, stands statue-like in its impassiveness toward God until "the Spirit giveth life." [1]

The possibility of life, indeed, is there. The soul is not an unconscious marble, it is not a senseless thing; it has latent capacities for love, truth, virtue—in one word, for holiness—which being roused would make it alive unto God. Yet education and appeal fail to call forth these powers until the Holy Ghost brings truth to the mind as light, and the light coming with the power of this divine actinism produces effects upon the soul that are like a new creation. A pupil may play a sonata of Beethoven correctly with

[1] 2 Cor. iii. 6.

respect to notes and time, but when the master touches the keys the soul of the composer enters into them and causes them to speak his thoughts. And the divine Spirit can so touch the native chords of feeling in the soul, that where hitherto there have been but formal mechanical utterances or a deadness of sound, there shall now be voiced forth heavenly truth and harmony. How this is effected we may not understand.

When we receive in New York a telegram from San Francisco, we do not question that it has crossed the continent, nor doubt the reality of the electric force, because we cannot see the fluid as it traverses the wires. So when we see the soul quickened by the message of God, it is not needed that we should see the operation of the Holy Spirit before accepting the fact and its result. And all the phenomena of regeneration teach, that did not the Spirit bring the truth into quickening contact with the soul, the Word of God itself would lie silent as the cable in the depths of the sea.

(2.) The Spirit by his gracious presence in the soul keeps in constant activity the principle of holiness which is "the power of an endless life." The voluntary adoption of the will of God as the supreme law of the soul, the yielding of the heart to God in a loving obedience, is the new life into which the soul is born through "the renewing of the Holy Ghost."[1] But this new principle, in its incipiency, may be much hindered, if not overborne, by habits long subservient to the flesh. It is to those whose minds are already renewed, and who have adopted the true law of spiritual life, that the admonition is yet addressed, "if ye live after the flesh, ye shall die."[2]

The reactionary tendency of carnal desires cannot be overcome by mere force of resolution. But the purpose to subdue those desires unto the new law of life is made effective through the co-working of the Holy Spirit. "The Spirit helpeth our infirmities"[3]—takes hold with us to bear us

[1] Titus iii. 5. [2] Rom. viii. 13. [3] Rom. viii. 26.

along, to carry us through—and "if we *through the Spirit* do mortify the deeds of the body, we shall live."[1] The principle of holiness, which springs up within the soul in the act of conversion, is kept alive and strengthened and at last made dominant over the flesh, by the Spirit of God dwelling in us.[2] Nearer than the counsel of a father interposed to restrain a child from wrong, or to nerve him for the right, nearer than the presence or the memory of a mother whose look is often the solvent of doubts and fears and the inspiration of hope and love, is the suggestion, the incitement, the kindling presence of the Paraclete within the soul, searching the things of a man with the deep things of God. Rightly to believe this, is to know it. To doubt this, is to call in question the omniscience and the omnipresence of the divine Spirit, and his yearning for the spiritual life of his children. Shall we refuse to live in the Spirit because we cannot comprehend what life is?

[1] Rom. viii. 13. [2] Rom. viii. 9.

CHAPTER VII.

THE HOLY SPIRIT AS DYNAMIC POWER.

The Working-energy of Believers.

"YE shall receive power after that the Holy Ghost is come upon you"[1] was the promise of Jesus at his ascension; and the promise was fulfilled to the first disciples on the day of Pentecost. Besides the power of the Holy Spirit upon the soul in its regeneration and sanctification, there is a power from the Spirit communicated to the believing soul which makes that soul a special, and at times even a supernatural, power in the world. This *dunamis* was not strictly the power of working miracles, for the apostles had already "power

[1] Acts i. 8.

and authority over all devils, and to cure diseases;"[1] but it was a power that should pertain to their personality through a participation of the Holy Ghost; a power expressly fitting them to propagate the Gospel as "witnesses"[2] for Christ. I call it *dynamic* to denote that it conveyed to the minds that received it a special motive-power or energy in the Christian work. To its first recipients the coming of this power was attested by miracles, and the miracles which they afterwards wrought are classified as "powers"[3] among the gifts of the Holy Spirit—a certain dynamic energy from the Holy Spirit giving them power over the forms and laws of the material world.

Power is an attribute of person. Spirits are powers as distinguished from things, from effects and from laws. Within the limitations of finite being, they can both originate and execute. And the divine

[1] Luke ix. 1 and x. 17. [2] Acts i. 8. [3] 1 Cor. xii. 10, *dunameis*, the effect being put for the cause.

Spirit can and does communicate to holy souls a special power for the work of righteousness in the world, so that their holy living and doing, like the speech and preaching of Paul, are "in demonstration of the Spirit and of power,"[1] *i.e.*, of the dynamic energy of the Holy Ghost. It is not necessary to the reality of such power that it be ostensible to the senses. The rushing wind that shook, as by earthquake, the house in Jerusalem; the cloven flame that played about the heads of the disciples; the sudden inspiration of different tongues, reversing the miracle at Babel—these all were but outward symbols of the Holy Ghost. His power entered dynamically into the souls of the disciples.

The Silence of Divine Forces.

POWER is measured not by noise nor outward signs, but by efficiency, the capacity to produce effects. Even in physical

[1] 1 Cor. ii. 4.

dynamics the most effective forces are often secret and silent. There is no visible machinery of the heavens, no apparatus of cogs, cranks, bands, wheels, by which the planets are guided in their courses; yet these enormous masses of matter move on, year after year, age after age, without danger of collision, and without moving a hair's-breadth from their appointed place. The force or law of gravitation is silent and invisible.

We cannot see the cold. We cannot tell what it is, but call it the absence of caloric —which is only defining in a circle. But "who can stand before his cold"?[1] Silent and invisible the frost steals over the face of the earth. It sinks down into the soil and makes it as a bed of rock or iron; it touches the roots of plants and they die; it chains the rivers; it binds even the restless waves of the sea; it stops the flow of water to our dwellings; it stops the commerce and the travel of the world; it snaps

[1] Psalm cxlvii. 17.

the iron rail, and makes the huge frame of the locomotive as crisp and brittle as a toy; it breaks in sunder bars of brass and steel; it cracks the iron girders of floors and roofs, and tumbles stores and depots into ruin. We philosophize upon it as the result of an irregular contraction and expansion—an uneven congelation of particles; but the force that thus masters all human works, and puts the vitality of nature under its ban, is itself noiseless and invisible. It cometh not with observation; but its reality is shown by its efficiency.

How silent falls the rain! A multitude of tiny drops, falling one by one—each too small to hurt an infant's head—scarce wetting the pavement under your feet—they give you no idea of force. But let it rain and rain and rain, hour after hour, day after day; the icy fetters are dissolved; that which man could not cut nor break, slowly melts away; the frozen earth grows moist again; the floods lift up their voice; the rivers burst their bonds, and bridges, fences, barns, houses, stock, merchandize, are borne on the resistless tide of tiny drops. Cities are submerged, and men stand aghast before the sudden and mighty force.

The returning sun touches the Arctic zone, and the fields of ice which steam could not penetrate, become an open sea! Yet what is heat? And what gives this marvellous power to the calorific rays of the sun? Once more our philosophy sends us round and round in the defining circle. Heat is caloric and caloric is heat, and cold is the sensation produced by the loss of caloric or heat. But the reality we know by its effects. Ah, these silent invisible forces, which we cannot grasp or measure or define!—more than the thunder, the whirlwind or the storm, are these the demonstration of power. Even so with the energy of the Holy Ghost. We may not have the earthquake, the flame, the tongues, the rushing wind, but we may receive the dynamic power, if, with a believing heart, we will receive the Holy Ghost.

Pascal has said that "God has established prayer in order to communicate to his creatures the dignity of causality, and in order to remind us from whom we have power." If by prayer we are in living communion with the Holy Ghost, we shall ourselves become powers, having causality in the spiritual world, working together with God, and approving ourselves as his servants, "by pureness, by knowledge, by long-suffering, by kindness, by the Holy Ghost, by love unfeigned, by the word of truth, by the power of God."[1]

[1] 2 Cor. vi. 1–8.

CHAPTER VIII.

THE HOLY SPIRIT AS A PLENARY PRESENCE.

The Pentecost his Advent.

THE manifestation of the Holy Spirit under the New Testament is of the character of a plenary and abiding presence. Under the Old Testament the distinct gifts of the Holy Spirit to believers, so far as these are recorded, were occasional and limited. Yet there was a prophetic promise that the pouring out of the Spirit upon the Church with plenitude and universality, should usher in the new era of the Messiah. That promise was fulfilled upon the day of Pentecost, when the Holy Ghost came upon all the disciples with diversity of gifts and plenitude of power, and came to abide in the Church.

The true significance of the miracle of Pentecost was not a manifestation of the Spirit once for all time—as the crucifixion of our Lord was an atoning sacrifice made once for all; the Pentecost was not merely the inauguration of the new religion; it was the pledge and sign that the Holy Spirit had come into the world according to the promise of Christ, thenceforth to use his direct, personal, complete and constant agency in carrying forward the work of redeeming grace in the hearts of men. He is always in the world as the Spirit of conviction, attending with his power the truth and the providences of God, convincing men of the guilt of sin, the need of righteousness, the reality of judgment and retribution. He is in the world as the Spirit of truth—a living spirit within the truth he has indited—illumining the sacred page with his own light, and purging the believing soul of darkness and error, that he may guide it into all truth. He is in the world as the Spirit of holiness, sanctifying the heart by his presence and power, so that they who taste this heavenly gift are "made partakers of the Holy Ghost and are sealed unto the day of redemption."[1] He is in the world as the Spirit of adoption, bearing witness with our spirit that we are the children of God. He is in the world as the Spirit of grace and supplications, making intercession for the saints according to the will of God. He is in the world as the Spirit of consolation, the Comforter, enabling tried and sorrowing saints to walk in the comfort of the gospel. He is in the world as the Spirit of wisdom. He "searcheth all things, yea the deep things of God;"[2] and by his illuminating power helps us to discern those spiritual realities that bring to us the very mind of Christ. He is in the world as the Spirit of life, making us free from the law of sin and death. Yea, He is in us as the power of an endless life; for "He that raised up Christ from the dead shall also quicken our

[1] Heb. vi. 11. [2] Cor. ii. 10.

mortal bodies by his Spirit that dwelleth in us."[1]

All this plenitude of spiritual offices and gifts, is with us always through the abiding presence of the Paraclete. In the first age of the Church, following the manifestation at the Pentecost, there were special modes of the Spirit's working which were meant to be transient. These had to do with establishing Christianity as a divine revelation by supernatural signs, and were not designed to be permanent accompaniments of Christianity or a part of its regular working agency.

Miracles not the Highest Gifts.

MIRACULOUS gifts were not confined to the apostles, but were widely shared by believers during the apostolic age. In the church at Corinth, one had gifts of healing; another had the general power of

[1] Rom. viii. 11.

working miracles; another, power to foretell the future; another, power to discern spirits, whether to read character, as Peter read Ananias and Simon Magus, or to detect evil spirits, as Paul detected the spirit of divination in the woman of Philippi; another, the gift of speaking in many tongues; another was empowered to interpret unknown tongues. These miraculous gifts seem to have continued in force, more or less, throughout the first century or the apostolic age, but gradually subsided as Christianity gained a foothold in the moral consciousness of the world. Viewed in the distance, they appear very superior as evidences of Christianity, and very fascinating as gifts or powers to be used for its advancement. In moments of ecstatic fervor, when religious contemplation grows imaginative and seems transfigured into vision, we may think the first disciples enviable because of these supernatural gifts, and fancy that could we rise a little higher in our own experience, we could grasp the same gifts and wield the same powers. In almost every age some have professed to have attained to the miraculous endowments of the Spirit—like Irving with his gift of tongues, or Müller with his wonder-working prayers—and some devout persons imagine that the age of miracles would return, if only there were enough of spirituality and faith among Christians to permit it. But why should it return? Is there any conceivable advantage to Christianity in respect either to evidences or to moral power, to be anticipated from a return of the age of miracles?

I hesitate not to say that any respectable church of modern times is superior to the church of Corinth in true moral power. Indeed I should be loth to minister to such a sorry set of Christians as were the Corinthians, with all their miracles and tongues. Wrangling about Paul, Apollos, and Cephas, running after false teachers, full of envying, strife and division, harboring an incestuous person without discipline, degrading the Lord's Supper into a feast of appetite, giving to Paul constant sorrow and anxiety, the Corinthians needed miracles to give them a respectable title to the Christian name; and they so abused miraculous gifts by jealousy and contention, that they turned their Sabbath assemblies into cabals of men and women shouting, singing, praying, prophesying, pell-mell, without decency or order. I have no desire to return to that age of Christianity with all its miracles. No doubt these Corinthians, converted pagans, ignorant and rude, with all their errors and defects, were true Christians, and the Spirit worked through them to give Christianity a footing in the world of Grecian idolatry and corruption. Yet the *miraculous* gifts of the Spirit were not evidences of extraordinary piety in their recipients, nor the divine seals upon a spirituality and a faith since departed.

Nor are such gifts to be looked for or even desired, as if they belonged to some higher dispensation of the Spirit in the future;

but the spiritual gifts which we all may enjoy by faith, are higher in value and in testimony than were those miraculous powers. In the Corinthian church itself, Paul placed the intellectual and moral expounders of Christianity above the rank of miracles, gifts of healing, diversities of tongues. "Tongues are for a sign to them that believe not;"[1] an outward evidence of supernatural power to convince the world of the divine origin of Christianity. But when Christianity had gained foothold in the world as a moral power, it was thenceforth greater in life and doctrine than in outward miracles. Hence miracles subsided, not through a decline of faith and piety, but because faith and piety had grown into a permanent living power for the moral conviction of the world.

"Five words spoken with the understanding," for the intelligent, hearty exposition of the gospel, teaching others also, are better than "ten thousand words in an un-

[1] Cor. xiv. 22.

known tongue."[1] Paul sets forth as the best gifts, those to be earnestly coveted, not miracles, nor inspired tongues, not the unusual and wonderful signs of the Spirit, but, morally, the spirit of charity, a large, earnest, sincere, catholic, working love; and next, spiritually, that enlightenment of the mind in the things of Christ which enables one to speak to men unto edification, exhortation, and comfort — these are the best gifts; the best fruits of the Spirit; worth more in these days for the proof of Christianity, than would be the dreams and visions, miracles and tongues of former times. We misconceive the dispensation of the Spirit, we dishonor his best work, when we crave to be seers and miracle-mongers, instead of studying to be holy exemplars of truth and love.

Setting aside then the outward miracles, which ceased when they had served their purpose of attesting and certifying Christianity, we find in the essence of the Spirit's

[1] 1 Cor. xiv. 19.

advent at Pentecost, a pledge and a type of his whole dispensation under the gospel.

The Spirit has already come.

THE Holy Spirit is not a vibratory medium between heaven and earth, oscillating in his movements according to the temperature of our spiritual frames. He is not continually coming and going; since by the original promise of his coming he came "to abide" with the disciples of Jesus "forever,"[1] came to "dwell" in the church, making it "a habitation of God through the Spirit."[2] If therefore we are indeed the children of God, that which we need for increase in the enjoyment of the Christian life and in the manifestation of spiritual power is not that the Holy Spirit should come to us, as if from heaven or from afar, but that we should come to him, come to the realization of his presence through a higher consciousness of the truth that he unfolds, and the

[1] John xiv. 16. [2] Eph. ii. 22.

love that he imparts, and through cherishing that purity with which he dwells.

This plenary presence of the Holy Spirit in the world since the day of Pentecost, is a peculiar glory of the New Testament dispensation. The prophets of the Old Testament had pointed to the plenary outpouring of the Spirit as a note of the beginning of the new era of the Messiah. The Apostle Peter declared the manifestation of the Spirit at the Pentecost to be the fulfilment of that prophecy. "The Holy Ghost had thus far only temporarily and sporadically visited the world, to enlighten certain specially favored individuals, the bearers of the Old Testament revelation. Now he took up his permanent abode upon earth to reside and work in the community of believers, as the principle of divine light and life, to apply more and more deeply and extensively to the souls of men the redemption objectively wrought by Christ."[1] This plenary

[1] Dr. Philip Schaff. History of the Apostolic Church, p. 191.

advent of the Spirit corresponded to the incarnation of Christ as a manifestation of the presence of God with men. It was the rehabilitation of the divinity in the world under a spiritual instead of a fleshly form. Peter furthermore declared it to be the fulfillment of the parting promise of Jesus to his disciples, that he would send them another Comforter: "being by the right hand of God exalted, and having received of the Father the promise of the Holy Ghost, he hath shed forth this which ye now see and hear."[1] But that promise was that the Holy Spirit should come to abide with the disciples forever; it was a promise not to the twelve, personally, but to them as disciples, and consecutively to all disciples. It was a coming which by the permanence and universality of its manifestations should compensate for the absence of the visible Saviour. The demonstration of the Spirit as a plenary presence on the day of Pentecost was "not an isolated and transient oc-

[1] Acts ii. 33.

currence, but the generative beginning of a vast series of workings and manifestations of God in history—the fountain of a river of life, which flows with unbroken current through all time, till it merge in eternity."[1]

After that manifestation the New Testament no more speaks of the "outpouring" of the Spirit, or of the "coming" of the Spirit, as blessings to be sought in prayer or looked for in the future of the Church. Such expressions are used only with reference to certain transient communications of miraculous powers;[2]—but the wondrous, glorious truth that the Holy Spirit had come into the world, and had made believing souls his habitation, is continually recognized for the comfort, the encouragement, the admonition, the quickening, the sanctification of the disciples of Christ. "The Spirit beareth witness with our spirit that we are children of God."[3] "Because we are sons, God hath sent forth the Spirit

[1] Schaff. Apostolic Church, p. 191.
[2] See the following section. [3] Rom. viii. 16.

of his Son into our hearts, crying Abba, Father."[1] By the Spirit we "have access unto the Father."[2] "The fruit of the Spirit is in all goodness, and righteousness and truth."[3] "If we love one another, God dwelleth in us, and his love is perfected in us. Hereby know we that we dwell in him, and he in us, because he hath given us of his Spirit."[4] To all true believers the Holy Ghost is now present with the plenitude of his gifts. What was the occasional inspiration of the Hebrew prophet concerning things to come, what the gift of miracles, at distant intervals, to the favored few, compared with this plenary presence of the Holy Spirit for our every use and necessity? How awful, how blessed, how inspiring the thought that God in the person of the Holy Ghost is ever with us, ever in the world prosecuting to a successful result in human souls the work of redemption accomplished through the incarnation and

[1] Gal. iv. 6. [2] Eph. ii. 18. [3] Eph. v. 9.
[4] 1 John iv. 12, 13.

sacrifice of the Son. How carefully and holily should we live, and yet how trustfully and joyfully withal, did we recognize this constant ministration of the Spirit. How earnestly and hopefully should we speak the truth of God in the ear of an unbelieving world, did we realize that the Holy Ghost, who came with such power of conviction on the day of Pentecost, is with us alway. How grand would be the faith, how sublime the energy of the Church of God did she live in the consciousness of the plenary presence of the Holy Ghost!

It is the transient awakening of this consciousness that gives a seeming periodicity to "revivals of religion." The Government and Constitution of the United States were ever present as latent powers, and were recognized by occasional acts of loyalty; but when war was made upon the flag of the nation, millions came to an instantaneous realization of their presence and authority as never before felt: and so the sudden shifting by the hand of Providence of material scenes that hinder spiritual perceptions may cause such a realization of the presence and power of the Holy Ghost that a nation shall be born in a day.

The Holy Spirit in Revivals.

THE presence of the Holy Spirit with the Church is not intermittent but abiding. "He that believeth in me," said Jesus, "out of his belly shall flow rivers of living water. But this spake he of the Spirit which they that believe on him should receive, for the Holy Ghost was not yet given, because that Jesus was not yet glorified."[1] This clearly implies that after the return of our Lord to the glory which he had with the Father, the Spirit would be given to his disciples in a manner which would mark his coming as an epoch. The Holy Ghost was thus "given" upon the Day of Pentecost.

In the progressive economy of redemp-

[1] John vii. 38, 39.

tion, the Father first manifested himself in the promise to Adam, in the covenant with Abraham, and in the law given at Sinai. After the work of preparation was accomplished, "when the fullness of the time was come, God sent forth his Son, made of a woman, made under the law, to redeem them that were under the law, that we might receive the adoption of sons."[1] There were intimations of Christ under the Old Testament, and some suppose that it was he who appeared in the early theophanies. But his "coming" was through the incarnation.

In like manner the Holy Spirit was active under the old dispensation, as the inspirer of prophecy and the sanctifier of the penitent; but he was not yet manifested in the world as a distinct Person of the Godhead performing a special work in the redemption of our race. In the divine plan this manifestation was withheld until the end of Christ's incarnation should be accomplished. It was announced upon the eve of

[1] Gal. iv. 4, 5.

his crucifixion, and it came to pass after Jesus was glorified. The Holy Ghost was then "given" to the body of Christ upon earth—to the household of faith—thenceforth to be in all prayers and praises, in all ministrations and sacraments, in all gifts, graces and labors, as the abiding Paraclete. An occasional, periodical, spasmodic piety, to which the Holy Spirit is now present, now absent, now near and urgent, now in heaven to be invoked, was not in the contemplation of that dispensation of the Spirit which began with his coming at Pentecost. Neither the renewed soul nor the spiritual church should be as a garden whose fruitfulness is dependent upon occasional showers, but should have within itself rivers of water bearing a continual freshness and life from the indwelling Spirit of God.

After the day of Pentecost we find in the Book of Acts four instances in which the Holy Ghost is said to have "come," to have "fallen," to have been "poured" out; but in each of these this language is used to describe the impartation of supernatural gifts, attested by notable signs, such as speaking with tongues and prophesying;[1] while with respect to the work of conviction and of sanctification, to all that pertains to the spiritual advancement of the kingdom of Christ, the Holy Spirit is represented as in the world always for these very ends. Such terms as "coming," "outpouring," and the like, may be used poetically, metaphorically, to denote some higher manifestation of his presence, some deeper consciousness of his power; but these should never betray us into the feeling that the Holy Spirit ever ceases to be in the world by his personal presence, caring for the kingdom of holiness. So true is that saying of Irenæus, "where the church is, there is also the Spirit of God; and where the Spirit of God is, there is the church."[2]

[1] See Acts. viii. 13–21. x. 44–47. xi. 15–18. xix. 2–6.

[2] Irenæus *adv. Hæreses*, Lib. III., xxxviii. 1.

Of Extraordinary Manifestations.

THIS doctrine of the plenary presence of the Holy Spirit is in entire harmony with seasons of extraordinary religious interest in churches or communities, known as revivals or "times of refreshing." As the Providence of God, which is both universal and particular, at times so manifests itself that men regard it as a special, almost a miraculous interposition, as sickness or death which are always from his hand will impress men as special judgments when they sweep over nations in the mysterious waves of pestilence or the horrid blasts of war, so the Holy Spirit though always present and always active for the truth, may use these same providences for his own impressions, or may shift the scenes of the spiritual world and make men suddenly conscious of realities which are near at every moment. The divine government of the universe, both physical and spiritual, includes what to human view is special and occasional, in perfect harmony with what men see to be general and uniform laws.

Moreover, human temperaments, sympathies, dispositions, occupations are variable; and hence there will always be "times and seasons" more favorable than others to concentrated, sustained, and elevated religious impressions. We should be wise to improve such opportunities, and all the more because we do not need to go about in quest of the Holy Spirit, nor to plead with God as if he were reluctant to bless, but because the Spirit is in the world in his plenary presence, and these very tokens of awakening are proof of that fact. Hence we should not direct our prayers and labors toward a revival as an end, but should endeavor to realize more fully the presence of the Spirit and pray for the demonstration of his power.

A Difficulty Relieved.

BUT some will say, "We have often prayed for the conversion of persons dear to us, and for the reviving of religion in our church and neighborhood, and have received no answer. How could this be if the Spirit is always present in his fullness for the work of conviction and regeneration?" The apostle teaches that prayer in accordance with the will of God is always answered in the fact that it is heard. "This is the confidence that we have in him, that, if we ask anything according to his will, he heareth us; and if we know that he hear us, whatsoever we ask, we know that we have the petitions that we desired of him."[1] Hence some infer that in the cases just instanced, either they have not prayed aright, or the subject of their prayers was not in accordance with the will of God. Yet neither inference may be warranted. It may be that you have prayed sincerely and in faith; it may be also, that the thing desired, the conversion of a friend, the reviving of religion, is in accordance with the *moral* preference or desire of God, who, in that sense, "will have all men to be saved

[1] 1 John v. 14, 15.

and to come unto the knowledge of the truth."[1] But it is not, it cannot be, according to the will of God to violate the fundamental laws of moral being, to annihilate in man that power of choice which may be used even in resisting God. It may be that God hears your prayers, that the Holy Spirit does convince your friend of sin ; but notwithstanding all your pleading and all the striving of the Spirit, that friend *will not come* to Christ that he might have life.[2] Whatever the laws or methods by which the Holy Spirit works upon the human soul, he will not subvert the moral constitution of the soul nor destroy the responsibility of the man for his own salvation or perdition. If therefore there be no present revival and no specific conversion, we should still pray in the faith that God hears us, and that the Holy Spirit is in the believing soul as a plenary presence and a dynamic power.

[1] 1 Tim. ii. 4. [2] John v. 40.

CHAPTER IX.

THE TEMPLE OF THE SPIRIT.

He dwells in the Church.

THE presence of the Spirit is in a manner localized in the Church. The dwelling of God with his people which, under the old dispensation was symbolized by the material temple with its ark of the covenant in the most holy place, is actualized under the new dispensation, in the Church—the collective body of believers, who by virtue of their personal union with Christ, are "builded together for a habitation of God through the Spirit."[1] This divine inhabitation of a body which is not corporate nor territorial, but spiritual and universal, declares in the most impressive manner the spirituality and universality of the religion of the New Tes-

[1] Eph. ii. 22.

tament in contrast with the ceremonial and national features of the Jewish dispensation. The Jewish Temple was not only sacred as to the locality, the building and the divine proprietorship therein, but restricted also in various degrees as to the privilege of worshipers, by nationality, sex and tribe. The Holy of Holies, the highest and innermost sanctuary, could be entered by the high priest alone, and by him only on the great day of atonement, once a year. It was death for any other person to enter it, or for him to enter it at any other time. Before this sanctuary was "the court of the priests," and the altar at which the sons of Levi ministered in the daily worship; and surrounding this "the court of Israel," into which only male Jews, ceremonially pure, could enter. In front of this again, and at a lower level was the "court of the women;"—not for women exclusively, since the men must cross it to enter their court—but so called because women were forbidden to go up the steps to the court of Israel and of the priests ; and below and in front of this court of the women — the "outer court" of the temple, just within the walls of the enclosure, but at the farthest remove from the sacred building—was "the court of the Gentiles," into which proselytes from the heathen to the Jewish faith might come to worship and bring their gifts. No person, who for any reason given in the Levitical law was ceremonially unclean, could pass even the outer gate of the sacred enclosure. The heathen proselyte, having been initiated into the Jewish faith, could enter the first court of the consecrated area. But between this court and that of the women, was not only the platform elevated by several steps, but a balustrade with pillars at intervals bearing an inscription in various languages, forbidding foreigners to advance into this sacred court under penalty of death. A mob was raised against Paul at Jerusalem, by the cry that he had taken Greeks into the temple and had polluted the holy place.

Such were the limitations under which the Jewish law of purity placed the Gentile worshiper at the temple-gate. He could stand in the lower and outer court, and looking up beyond successive courts and walls and flights of consecrated steps, might see afar off that holy place where was enshrined the ark of God's covenant with Israel. Both national birthright and ceremonial purity were needed as qualifications for the full privileges of the temple-worship.

But the dispensation of the Gospel abolishes nationality and ceremonialism from the sphere of religion, and introduces a spiritual power and privilege, of equal and universal application.

The epistle to the Ephesians teaches that believers collectively constitute "a holy temple in the Lord;" in whom they all are "fitly framed together"[1] as one building. And with reference to the national and ceremonial distinctions of the old temple wor-

[1] Eph. ii. 21.

ship, the apostle wrote to these Gentile converts, "In time past ye were aliens from the commonwealth of Israel, and strangers from the covenants of promise; but now in Christ Jesus, ye who were far off, are made nigh by the blood of Christ, who hath broken down the middle wall of partition between us"[1]—that old temple wall which separated Jews from Gentiles in their worship—"for through him we both have an access by one Spirit unto the Father. Now therefore, ye are no more strangers and foreigners, but fellow-citizens with the saints, and of the household of God."[2] And not only are they within the temple, having equal privileges of worship, but they are of the temple, as constituent parts of that spiritual house, the Church of Christ, which takes the place of the old material temple as the seat of God's glory and grace in redemption. "For ye are built upon the foundation of the apostles and prophets, Jesus Christ himself being the chief corner-

[1] Eph. ii. 14. [2] Eph. ii. 18, 19.

stone; in whom ye also are builded together"—these very Jews and Gentiles once separated in the temple itself by walls of partition, walls of race, walls of prejudice, walls of caste—they are not brought only together by Christ, but are *builded* together *in* Christ, "for a habitation of God through the Spirit." How sublime this conception of the spirituality, the unity, the holy blessedness of the Church of God!

Every Christian a Temple.

NOT only is the aggregate fellowship of Christian believers the sphere in which God manifests his sanctifying presence and grace as in the temple of old; not only does the totality of believers which is the true body of Christ, enjoy that peculiar glory of the divine presence which is no longer given to any place or building upon earth; but each individual Christian is himself a temple of the Holy Ghost, a "habitation of God through the Spirit."[1] The Gentile who could only stand in the lowest, outermost court of the Jewish temple, and look with timid glances toward the Holy of Holies, which he might not venture to approach, is himself the temple of God's presence, consecrated to his service, and made holy by the indwelling of his Spirit. All of sacredness and glory that the presence of Jehovah imparted to the temple on Moriah, is now brought to the believer himself through the consecrating gift and presence of the Spirit; and the realization of this dwelling of the Spirit within us as his temple, is the highest perfection of being, the highest conception of fellowship with God, the highest measure of spiritual life and power, the highest blessedness in religion possible to the human mind, until, with spiritualized and glorified bodies we shall inhabit that world where "there is no temple, for the Lord God Almighty and the Lamb are the temple of it."[2]

[1] Eph. ii. 22. [2] Rev. xxi. 22.

Neither Pantheistic nor Mystical.

THIS doctrine of the divine inhabitation of the souls of believers is altogether different from the Pantheistic notion that God is in man, is in nature, is in the universe as a soul or a spiritual force, just as the principle of life is in our bodies. Pantheism leaves out of view the personality and the holiness of God, and makes his presence like the law of gravitation in the heavenly bodies, like the vital force in living creatures, like the sap in a tree—a controlling power or influence acting upon the material organism. But the Biblical doctrine of the indwelling of the Spirit is not that a supernatural power takes forcible possession of the bodily organization, according to the notion of "spiritual possession" held by Mohammedan dervishes and Hindoo devotees, nor that a vague, impersonal influence from the Deity pervades and actuates the human spirit, but that the Holy

Spirit purifies and controls the body through a renovated soul. That the Spirit is a person, that he is holy, and that he aims to produce holiness in men, are essential points in the Bible doctrine of his indwelling.

On the other hand, there is a mystical notion that the Holy Spirit, as an essence, somehow dwells in the innermost heart of a renewed man as in a shrine, quite apart from the man himself and his mental and moral acts—a mysterious entity, of whose presence the mind is vaguely conscious as a something distinct from itself, and which acts upon the mind in the way of direct inspiration, impulse, vision, or spiritual exaltation; that is to say, the Spirit's indwelling is a mysterious something that produces certain supernatural frames and experiences within the soul apart from the normal action of its own faculties. But the Bible represents this indwelling neither as physical nor as fanciful; neither as a power acting upon the nerves and organs of the body, nor a light, a voice, a mystery addressing the imagination; but as the personal influence of the Holy Spirit upon the will and the affections, inciting and disposing these to holy love and holy living. Whatever the influence of the Spirit upon the man, it is directed to the renovation and sanctification of his moral nature. Hence we must keep always in view the nature of the substance upon which the Spirit acts, namely, the immaterial, intelligent, voluntary soul; and, as says John Howe, "Because it was a *rational subject* that was to be wrought upon, it is also to be expected that the work itself be done in a *rational way*. Now, the forcing of a man's will implies a contradiction in the terms; for we have no other notion of force than the making one do a thing against his will. But it is impossible a man should will or be willing *against* his will."[1]

The Holy Spirit acts on the body only through the soul, which guides and controls

[1] Howe's Living Temple; Works, Bohn's edition, pp. 80 and 101.

the body; and it acts upon the soul only through the proper laws of its being—leading, inciting, sustaining it in the choice and practice of what is true, lovely, pure, excellent, noble, godlike. When the will thus comes into harmony with the will of God, loving holiness and seeking truth and righteousness, then the divine Spirit is said to enter into a man; and when this devotion to the will of God is continuous, as the purpose and habit of the soul, then the Holy Spirit is said to dwell in the man. And since he who thus devotes himself to God will not seek his own pleasure, will deny ungodliness and worldly lusts, will "no more make provision for the flesh to fulfil the lusts thereof," but will "keep the body under," such a one is said, even in his body, to be a temple of the Holy Ghost; being consecrated in thought, word and act to the service of a holy God, and instead of yielding the mind to the control of carnal impulses and desires, regulating these by the higher law of life in the soul. "Ye are not in the flesh, but in the Spirit, if so be that the Spirit of God dwell in you."[1]

Analogy of the Temple.

"KNOW ye not that your body is the temple of the Holy Ghost which is in you, which ye have of God, and ye are not your own? For ye are bought with a price; therefore glorify God in your body and in your spirit, which are God's."[2] The analogy of the body of the believer to the temple is twofold. The temple was the dwelling-place of God in the symbols of his glory. Though the ark of the covenant was secluded from the common gaze in the Holy of Holies, yet the presence of that symbol in the oracle imparted a sacredness to the entire building, with its courts and appurtenances, so that nothing unclean might enter it. Upon certain occasions, as at the dedication, the splendor of the

[1] Rom. viii. 9. [2] 1 Cor. vi. 19, 20.

divine manifestation so awed and overpowered the priests, that they could not stand to minister because of it: For "the glory of the Lord filled the house of the Lord."[1]

Moreover, the temple, thus made sacred by the presence of Jehovah in the symbols of his grace and glory, was consecrated to him as a possession. It was a free-will offering from man to God. From the day of dedication Solomon had no title in the building; no proprietorship over it; no lien upon it; no reversionary interest in the land, the house, or its furniture. It was set apart from all human property and interests as a divine possession—"the house of the Lord forever;"—Jehovah, its alone proprietor, sanctifying it as his abode. When Manasseh set up an idol in the temple, he "polluted the house of the Lord;" when invaders carried away the vessels of the temple, this was the crime of sacrilege.

These two features of the Jewish temple were the basis of the analogy between that

[1] 1 Kings viii. 11.

temple and the body of the believer. As the temple was made sacred by the presence of Jehovah, so is the body of the believer made sacred by the indwelling of the Holy Ghost. "Know ye not that ye are the temple of God, and that the Spirit of God dwelleth in you? If any man defile the temple of God, him shall God destroy: for the temple of God is holy, which temple ye are."[1] And again, as the temple was consecrated to the service of Jehovah, so that its proprietorship was not in man, but in God, so they in whom the Spirit dwells are set apart as God's possession, consecrated not only by their act, but by his purchase of redemption. "Ye are not your own; ye are bought with a price." Therefore, the apostle argues, the believer should glorify God even in his body, as in a temple consecrated to his worship and employed only in his service. The gospel, so far from inculcating indifference toward the body, "honors the body as the permanent

[1] 1 Cor. iii. 16, 17.

organ of the soul, glorified with it through the Holy Spirit. The body is the dwelling, the temple of the soul; but the Holy Ghost, working in and on the soul, transforms it into his own nature, and thus dwells in the human body as in a temple;"[1] and since believers have been purchased by the blood of Christ, and are in the possession of the Holy Spirit as his temple, the apostle reminds them not only of the sanctity of the temple to be preserved, but of this divine proprictorship to be respected. "Ye belong no more to yourselves, that ye may govern yourselves by your own wills, but God is your Lord, and ye must be led by his Spirit. Know ye not that your body is the temple of the Holy Ghost, which is in you."[2]

This two-fold analogy suggests two principal conditions upon which the Holy Spirit thus abides in the believer. Since he gains possession of the soul only through the will yielding itself to his conviction and

[1] Olshausen, Com. on 1 Cor. vi. 18, 19. [2] Ibid.

persuasion, and placing itself under his guidance, and since he enters the soul for the one purpose of quickening, guiding, and sustaining it in the work of its own sanctification, so he will abide in the soul only on the condition that holiness is there cherished and advanced. Hence it is to Christians that the warning is given, "Grieve not the Holy Spirit of God, whereby ye are sealed unto the day of redemption." [1]

The soul must be kept from contamination through those desires of the flesh which have been the ministers of sin. Carnal-mindedness, whether in the grosser appetites and passions, or in the form of pride, vanity or any inordinate self-gratification, is directly contrary to the mind of the Spirit. He who lives to please himself cannot please God. The Scriptures lay stress especially upon the regulation of the *body* by Christian principle, as both a token and a condition of the Spirit's presence. The fruits of the Spirit are put in contrast with

[1] Eph. iv. 30.

the works of the flesh. "They that are Christ's have crucified the flesh with the affections and lusts."[1] "Walk in the Spirit and ye shall not fulfil the lust of the flesh. For the flesh lusteth against the Spirit, and the Spirit against the flesh, and these are contrary the one to the other."[2] "Abstain from fleshly lusts which war against the soul."[3] "Put off the old man which is corrupt according to the deceitful lusts, and be renewed in the spirit of your mind; and put on the new man, *i. e.*, a new character, spirit, and habit of life—which after God is created in righteousness and true holiness."[4] In the epistle to the Romans, this subjection of the body to the law of holiness is treated at much length, especially in the sixth, seventh and eighth chapters. "Let not sin reign in your mortal body, that ye should obey it in the lusts thereof. Neither yield ye your members as instruments of unrighteousness unto sin; but

[1] Gal. v. 24. [2] Gal. v. 17. [3] 1 Peter ii. 4.
[4] Eph. iv. 24.

yield yourselves unto God, as those that are alive from the dead, and your members as instruments of righteousness unto God."[1]

The analogy of the temple strikingly enforces watchfulness against the corruptions of the flesh. To profane or defile the temple was a crime worthy of death. The holy God would not dwell in a polluted sanctuary. "Know ye not that ye are the temple of God, and that the Spirit of God dwelleth in you? If any man defile the temple of God, him shall God destroy; for the temple of God is holy, which temple ye are."[2] "And what agreement hath the temple of God with idols? for ye are the temple of the living God. Wherefore come out from among them and be ye separate, and touch not the unclean thing."[3] "Having, therefore, these promises, let us cleanse ourselves from all filthiness of the flesh and spirit, perfecting holiness in the fear of God."[4]

[1] Rom. vi. 13. [2] 1 Cor. iii. 16, 17.
[3] 2 Cor. vi. 16, 17. [4] 2 Cor. vii. 1.

The other condition of the indwelling of the Spirit is the consecration of all our powers to God and their employment in his service. Following the analogy of the temple, there must be the dedication of ourselves to him as an abode, which implies watchfulness against all defilement of sin; and there must also be the consecration of ourselves to him as a possession, which implies the relinquishment of all selfish interests and claims. The conclusion of Paul from his grand exhibition of the goodness and grace of God in redemption is, "I beseech you, therefore, brethren, by the mercies of God, that ye present your *bodies* a living sacrifice, holy, acceptable to God, which is your reasonable service."[1] "Ye are not your own, ye are bought with a price."[2]

[1] Rom. xii. 1. [2] 1 Cor. vi. 19, 20.

Tokens of the Spirit's Indwelling.

SINCE the coming of the Spirit into the soul is not by way of visions, revelations, or other objective supernatural appearances, nor by means of ecstacies and like abnormal subjective phenomena, his presence is betokened, not by mysterious frames and impressions, but through that cardinal law of character which is laid down by the apostle: "They that are after the flesh, do mind the things of the flesh; but they that are after the Spirit, the things of the Spirit."[1] There are also specific fruits of the Spirit which are infallible tokens of his indwelling. "The fruit of Spirit is love, joy, peace, long suffering, gentleness, goodness, faith, meekness, temperance;"[2] this combination of virtues and graces so contrary to the selfish inclinations of men, argues a divine transformation of the spirit and temper of the soul; for

[1] Rom. viii. 5. [2] Gal v. 22.

though some of these virtues may be cultivated singly and to a limited extent by unrenewed minds, the combination of them all in one character, and their continuous manifestation in the life, is evidence that the mind is filled with the Spirit. Such evidence is surest in kind, and is permanent in its quality. Rhapsody may mislead and does not long abide. And no extraordinary illumination within the soul could compare for evidence with this steady, luminous quality of the soul itself, when the Spirit shines through its graces as through a transparency. The one is a sky-rocket, the other a constellation.

Yet there are internal evidences as well as external fruits of the indwelling of the Spirit; evidences which have no tincture of mysticism or of enthusiasm, but are as clear and reliable as are the tokens of health in the body. Since the Holy Spirit alone can produce in the mind of man a just and adequate conviction of sin—an enlightened conscientiousness may be taken as an evidence of his abiding in the soul; an *enlightened conscientiousness*—not merely an awakened conscience, for one may have that, who is resisting the Spirit; not a mere scrupulosity about outward acts, for that may be the very spirit of Pharisaism, will-worship or legality, a piety compounded of mint, anise and cummin, and omitting justice, mercy, faith, and the love of God; but a conscience so intelligently alive toward God and duty that it shrinks with the most sensitive aversion from the suggestion or shadow of sin, and looks for guidance not to the bit and bridle of the law, but to the pure, holy, loving eye of the Master. When conscience delights to place itself under the eye of God, this is a token of the presence of the Spirit in the soul. And, moreover, since it is the Holy Spirit who quickens the soul dead in trespasses and sins—making it alive with new motives, aims, principles and hopes—an honest, thorough, earnest, positive *love of holiness*, and the constant cultivation of holy affections and exercises, is a token that the Spirit has taken up his abode in the heart. Where its own sanctification for the glory of God is the supreme and constant desire of the soul, there is evidence of the highest kind that the Holy Spirit has made that soul his dwelling-place.

And for the same reasons, *a lively sense of the preciousness of things spiritual and divine*, and especially the preciousness of communion with God in Christ, is a token of the indwelling of the Spirit, since it is preëminently as the medium of filial, joyful, satisfying communication between the soul and God, that the Spirit abides in the soul that he renews. Wherever the heart that has renounced sin and has consecrated itself to God in Christ is moved with filial love and confidence to cry "Abba, Father," there the Holy Spirit witnesses his presence, making that heart the temple of his intercessions.

The Glory of this Indwelling.

THE true dignity and exaltation of humanity can come only through its inhabitation by the Spirit of God. The Epicurean philosophy pampered and abused the body because it was to perish at death. The Stoical philosophy despised and degraded the body, as a hindrance to the soul. Christianity discerns in the body a temple in ruins—a temple once glorious with the presence of God, the habitation of a soul made in God's image, and capable of being built again for a habitation of God through the Spirit. Therefore Christianity will neither worship the body nor despise it; but would renovate it for the abode of all heavenly graces, the glory of the Divine presence. This invests our humanity with a dignity that it could never assert for itself.

We count it a great advance in political philosophy that man as man is recognized as an integral part and power in the state. Yet the highest advance of political science in exalting the individual falls infinitely short of the teaching of Christianity on this point. Political science deals only with the human, the earthly, the transient. The essential rights of man, his intelligent personality and his moral nature, forbid that he should be subjected to violence and oppression when guiltless of crime. But when we conceive of a temple of the Holy Ghost set up on the auction-block to be knocked off to the highest bidder, there is a horror of that crime which no vaunting of human nature or of political freedom could inspire. The claims of God are outraged; the temple of God is defiled; it is the crime of sacrilege joined to blasphemy against the Holy Ghost!

Philanthropy is tame until we bring into view the glorious possibilities of human nature as renewed, possessed and occupied by the Spirit of God. If man is only a higher sort of animal, if his chief interests are those of time and sense, then the motive to care for him is proportionately low and narrow. "Multiply the epicure's paradise by the accumulated science of a thousand years, and I do not think it proves us a bit nearer the conversion of this earth into a kingdom of God. The invention of piquant sauces, luxurious furniture, tasteful jewelry, etc., I humbly decline to accept as proofs of anything, beyond the fact that man is a very sagacious and surprising beaver."[1] So of all social progression in the mere line of material interests; it is "of the earth, earthy." The "coming man" who is the ideal of the socialistic philosophy can be found only in the "new man" of the Gospel of Christ. The highest dignity of man is to be consciously a child of the Infinite Father, through the inhabitation of himself, body, soul and spirit, by the Holy Ghost.

This consecration of our humanity by the Spirit gives a glorious significance to

[1] F. W. Robertson, Letters, vol. ii. p. 51.

the Christian doctrine of the resurrection. Christ entered into our humanity not only to redeem and save, but to ennoble and glorify it. When death touched and destroyed the temple of his body, he raised it again on the third day, and was thus "declared to be the Son of God with power, according to the Spirit of holiness."[1] And now, in all his relations to the body and to death the Christian believer dates not from the first Adam, "of the earth, earthy," but from the second Adam, "the Lord from heaven—a quickening Spirit."[2] The body of the true believer is the temple of the Holy Ghost. Death may dishonor but shall not destroy it. The temple of the Holy Ghost shall be built again. "If the Spirit of him that raised up Jesus from the dead dwell in you, he that raised up Christ from the dead shall also quicken your mortal bodies by his Spirit that dwelleth in you. The working of the life-producing Spirit shall not stop at the purely spiritual resurrec-

[1] Romans i. 4. [2] Cor. xv. 45–48.

tion, nor at that of the body from dead works to serve the living God, but shall extend even to the building up the spiritual body in the future new and glorious life."[1]

[1] Alford, Com. on Romans viii. 11.

CHAPTER X.

THE TRINITY MANIFESTED BY THE SPIRIT.

The Baptismal Consecration.

AFTER his resurrection Jesus commanded his disciples to "teach all nations, baptizing them in the name of the Father, and of the Son, and of the Holy Ghost."[1] This, then, is the universal formula of Christian discipleship as given by the Lord Jesus Christ. Baptism under this form is the mode of initiation into the Christian Church; yet one may be baptized a disciple of Christ, as was the Ethiopian eunuch by Philip on the wayside, without thereby entering into communion with any particular Church.

It is also a symbolic rite setting forth the repentance and regeneration, or in one word,

[1] Matt. xxviii. 14.

the spiritual cleansing of the subject of it. Yet this does not exhaust its meaning, for John preached the baptism of repentance for the remission of sins, but his baptism, though it was a sign of spiritual cleansing and also of faith in the coming Messiah, was not *Christian* baptism ; and, hence the disciples at Ephesus who had received only John's baptism, were baptized again by Paul in the name of the Lord Jesus.

We must add to these ideas of initiation into the communion of saints and of symbolic cleansing from sin, which we associate with baptism, the further ideas of a declaration of faith and a vow of consecration in the form herein prescribed. Men are made disciples of Christ—openly recognized and declared his followers—by being baptized into the name of the Father, and of the Son, and of the Holy Ghost. To be baptized " into the name " of any one is to avow faith in him if he be a teacher, to pledge obedience to him if he be a leader. In this formula both elements are combined ;—the baptism is a declaration of belief, and a vow of consecration, or in a now current phrase, an "oath of allegiance." It is equivalent to this: "I, A. B., believing in the Father, and in the Son, and in the Holy Ghost, as revealed in the Scriptures, confessing and renouncing my sins, do give myself up to serve and honor that sacred Name with the allegiance of all my powers."

The formula of discipleship was prescribed by Christ himself, and is universal and perpetual. On the one hand, we are not at liberty to modify or omit it; and on the other, we must be careful to accept and to apply it in its whole and exact meaning. This formula of Christian discipleship is not simply a declaration of belief in God and of consecration to his service. When the people of Israel were convoked to enter into a national covenant with Jehovah, the solemnity began in this wise: "Hear, O Israel; the Lord our God is *one* Lord; and thou shalt love the Lord thy God with all thy heart, and with all thy soul, and with all thy might."[1] But this Christian formula brings in another element. It is no less important now than in the days of Israel that pagans should be converted from their belief in many gods, to a belief in the one only living and true God ; and yet the heathen upon becoming Christians are to be baptized, not simply in the name of Jehovah as the one Lord, but "in the name of the Father, and of the Son, and of the Holy Ghost."[2]

Moreover, this formula is not simply nor specifically a declaration of discipleship unto Christ, or of adherence to Christ personally as teacher, leader, Saviour. To accept Christ as the highest teacher, even as perfect and infallible in wisdom and in truth, to accept Christianity as the ultimate truth in morals and religion, and to be baptized into that faith and profession, does not come up to this formula of discipleship. The Israelites who went out of Egypt are said to have been "all baptized unto Moses in the

[1] Duet. vi. 4, 5. [2] Matt. xxviii. 19.

cloud and in the sea;"[1]—by following the pillar of cloud as Moses bade them, and at his word entering into the divided sea, they committed themselves as by a covenant of baptism to his guidance and authority. In like manner the disciples of Christ are baptized unto his leadership and authority—to observe all things whatsoever he has commanded;—but this avowal of Christ as our Master does not cover the whole extent of the formula of discipleship enjoined by Christ himself.

Nor is this formula exhausted by a declaration of faith in Christ as the representative of God to men, and in Christianity as a revelation divinely authenticated. The Musselman sums up his creed in the article that "there is no God but Allah, and Mohammed is his prophet." With true Moslems this declaration is their call to prayer and their battle-cry; their test of loyalty and their pledge of devotion. They may be said to be steeped in this as their

[1] Cor. x. 3.

faith. And so the Christian makes God revealed in Christ the essence of his faith, the substance of his hope, the power of his life — for "this is life eternal, that they might know thee, the only true God, and Jesus Christ whom thou hast sent."[1] Yet even this belief in the one true God and in Jesus Christ his ambassador of truth and grace, does not exhaust Christ's own formula of discipleship: "Go teach or make disciples of all nations, baptizing them in the name of the Father, and of the Son, and of the Holy Ghost." The baptism that Christ appointed for the initiation and recognition of his disciples is a declaration of faith in a three-fold yet common name, and a covenant of consecration unto "the Father, and the Son, and the Holy Ghost." The coming of the Holy Spirit made complete the manifestation of the Trinity, and the realization of the offices of the Trinity in the work of redemption.

[1] John xvii. 3.

The Trinity of the New Testament.

THE formula of Christian discipleship *discriminates* between the Father, the Son, and the Holy Ghost. Whoever or whatever these are, they are distinguished each from the others. Each is introduced with the definite article—*the* Father, *the* Son, *the* Holy Ghost, and they are linked together by the copulative *and*. Hence there is some ground or reason by which they are severally distinguished.

The three, Father, Son, and Holy Ghost, are *parallelized* in this formula. Though they are mentioned in a certain order, there is nothing in this that implies a descending series—the inferiority of either to another. On the contrary, by being linked together in the high and sacred formula whereby the believer declares his faith and enters into covenant, these three, the Father, the Son, and the Holy Ghost are set before us on a parallel as objects of that faith and parties to that covenant. And yet, while thus presented as distinct and as parallel we find that these three are *conjoined* in one name. The formula does not read "Baptizing them in the name of the Father, and in the name of the Son, and in the name of the Holy Ghost"—but in the one common name of the Father, and of the Son, and of the Holy Ghost. Whoever or whatever these terms signify, while each is distinguished by a separate title, the three are conjoined in one name as the object of faith and of allegiance in the act of baptism, that seals and certifies a Christian discipleship. Clearly then the formula of discipleship given by Christ postulates, in some sense, a TRINITY IN UNITY as the complete conception of the godhead. The name into which we as Christians are baptized, is the name of God; no inferior name, no other name can be assumed as that to which we bring our reverent homage, our adoring faith, our formal and spiritual consecration, through this sealing confession of discipleship. Yet in the formula itself the name given is not God or Jehovah, but the three-fold name of the Father, and of the Son, and of the Holy Ghost. Here, beyond a cavil, is a three-ness in one-ness.

Thus without recourse to metaphysical theology or to the historical dogmas of the Church, but by a simple and plain analysis of Christ's own words, we have come at the fact that in the *name* into which as Christians we are baptized, there is the Father, and the Son, and the Holy Ghost, distinguished each from the others, made parallel in this consecrating rite, and conjoined in one. And the same fact repeats itself substantially in the apostolic benediction:—"The grace of the Lord Jesus Christ, and the love of God, and the communion of the Holy Ghost, be with you all."[1] What then is the import of this fact? What is the Trinity set forth in the New Testament? or, in other words, what do the Scriptures teach concerning God in the mode of his existence?

[1] 2 Cor. xii. 14.

The Unity of God.

THE Bible teaches that there is one and only one God. This truth is declared uniformly, consistently and with emphasis, both in the Old Testament as a protest against polytheism, and in the New Testament as the basis of one universal faith and worship. It is proclaimed as an official declaration. "Hear, O Israel, the Lord our God is *one* Lord."[1] "O Lord God of Israel, which dwellest between the cherubims, thou art the God, even thou alone, of all the kingdoms of the earth; thou hast made heaven and earth."[2] The unity of God is proclaimed in promise and prophecy. "All nations whom thou hast made shall come and worship before thee, O Lord; and shall glorify thy name. For thou art great and doest wondrous things; thou art God alone."[3] "Thus saith the Lord the

[1] Deut. vi. 4. [2] 2 Kings xix. 15.
[3] Psalm lxxxvi. 9, 10.

king of Israel, and his Redeemer the Lord of hosts; I am the first and I am the last; and besides me there is no God. Is there a God besides me? Yea, there is no God."[1] Not to Israel only was this said, but to Cyrus the king of a nation of idolaters, whose heart was moved to do good to Israel, it was declared with repeated emphasis: "I am the Lord, and there is none else, there is no God besides me. . . . . . A just God and a Saviour; there is none besides me."[2]

Jesus reiterated this truth in his personal teaching. When asked, which is the first commandment, he answered: "The first of all the commandments is, Hear, O Israel, the Lord our God is one Lord; and thou shalt love the Lord thy God with all thy heart, and with all thy soul, and with all thy mind and with all thy strength;"[3] and he approved and endorsed the answer of the scribe; "Master, thou hast said the truth: for there is one God, and there is none other

[1] Isaiah xliv. 6, 8. [2] Isaiah xl. 21.
[3] Mark xii. 29.

but he."[1] And again Jesus in his prayer recorded by John, addresses his Father as "the only true God."[2] "We know," says Paul, "that an idol is nothing in the world, and that there is none other God but one. For though there be that are called gods, whether in heaven or in earth; to us there is but one God;"[3]—this truth lies at the foundation of the Christian faith and worship as it lay at the foundation of the Jewish religion and nationality. The apostle describes the conversion of the Gentiles as the "turning to God from idols, to serve the living and true God."[4] And not only is the truth that there is but one God thus positively and emphatically declared—but the recognition of any other God beside Jehovah is threatened with his extreme displeasure. "Thou shalt have no other gods before me, or beside me; for I the Lord thy God am a jealous God."[5] "Ye shall not fear other gods, nor bow yourselves to them,

[1] Mark xii. 32. [2] John xvii. 3. [3] 1 Cor. viii. 5, 6.
[4] 1 Thess. i. 9. [5] Ex. xx. 3–5.

nor sacrifice to them."[1] "Go not after other gods to serve them, and worship them, and provoke me not to anger with the works of your hands"[2] (*i. e.* with false divinities). "I am the Lord; that is my name; and my glory will I not give to another."[3] "Hearken unto me, O Jacob and Israel my called; I am he; I am the first, I also am the last. . . . . . My hand also hath laid the foundation of the earth, and my right hand hath spanned the heavens. . . . . . I will not give my glory unto another."[4]

Concerning the lapse of Israel into idolatry it is said "they provoked him to jealousy with strange gods, with abominations provoked they him to anger. And when the Lord saw it, he abhorred them. They have moved me to jealousy with that which is not God. See now that I, even I am he, and there is no God with me; I kill, and I make alive; I wound and I heal; neither is there any that can deliver out of my

[1] 2 Kings xvii. 35.
[2] Jer. xxv. 6.
[3] Isa. xlii. 8.
[4] Isa. xlviii. 14.

hand. For I lift up my hand to heaven, and say, I live forever."[1] "Thou shalt know no God but me."[2]

Hence the starting point in the Biblical doctrine of the Trinity, the point about which the whole subject must revolve, and to which every fact revealed concerning the mode of Divine existence must be adjusted, is that there is and can be, only one God; and the constituting more than one God in form or in thought, the acknowledging more than one Being as God, whether by a formal object of worship or a metaphysical dogma, is contrary to the Scriptures, and is specially abhorrent to him who is God alone. The bare conception of more than one God entertained as a reality, cherished as a belief, is an infringement upon his prerogative of self-existence, a detraction from his majesty and glory, which the God of the Bible denounces as the most offensive sin. It matters not whether we make three gods or the three hundred million gods of India, whether

[1] Deut. xxxii. 16, 19, 39. [2] Hosea xiii. 4.

we shape these divinities into idols or embody them in dogmas of theology—any departure from the strict idea that there is one only living and true God is unbiblical, unphilosophical, impious.

No Christian communion holds any other faith than this—that there is but ONE GOD; and therefore it is a wrong to the Church universal for any body of Christians to assume that the unity of God is an exclusive tenet of their theology; that the distinction between them and others is, that they believe in only one God. There is no such distinction. Whoever and whatever God is, wherever and however he exists, under whatever modes and conditions he is revealed, there is and can be but one such Being in the Universe. This is the faith of Christendom.

The Tri-personality.

WITH this fundamental truth of the Oneness of God, lying at the basis of the Christian revelation, we find also that in the New Testament, the Father is set before us with all the attributes of God; the Son is set before us with all the attributes of God; and the Holy Ghost is set before us with all the attributes of God; and in the most solemn acts and invocations of religion, the Father, the Son, and the Holy Ghost are made parallel. It is unnecessary to argue the divinity of the Father from texts of Scripture, since the "Father of spirits," the "Father of lights," the "Father of mercies," is acknowledged to be the infinite and absolute God. But the New Testament declares no less explicitly that the Word who "was made flesh and dwelt among us" was God;[1] that Christ who, "as concerning the flesh" came of "the fathers,"

[1] John i. 1.

is "over all God blessed forever."[1] He who was "made in the likeness of men, and became obedient unto death, even the death of the cross," was "in the form of God," and by this humiliation emptied himself, not insisting upon his own eternal prerogatives as the equal of God.[2] Jesus declared himself the Son of God, knowing that the Jews understood him as thus "making himself equal with God;"[3] and he accepted from Thomas the adoring homage, "My Lord and My God."[4]

Moreover all the proper attributes of divinity are ascribed to Christ. He is "the first and the last"[5]—therefore eternal; he is the "I AM;"[6] therefore infinite and self-existent; he searches the reins and hearts, and "knows what is in man,"[7] and is therefore omniscient; he has "all power in heaven and in earth," he rules the worlds of nature and of spirit, and raises the dead

[1] Romans ix. 5. [2] Ellicot on Phil. ii. 5–8.
[3] John v. 8, x. 30. [4] John xx. 28.
[5] Rev. i. 2. [6] John viii. 58. [7] Matt. xxv. 18.

—he is therefore omnipotent; he is "with his disciples always,"[1] therefore omnipresent; "all things were made by him,"[2] and he "upholdeth all things by the word of his power;"[3] he is the creator and preserver of the worlds; "in Him is life;"[4] "he only hath immortality;"[5] he has control, therefore, of the higher region of spiritual realities; he forgives sin, and he will "judge the world"[6]—he is therefore the moral governor of the universe; he is "alpha and omega, the beginning and the ending—the Lord which is, and which was, and which is to come, the Almighty,"[7] the "blessed and only Potentate, the King of kings, and the Lord of lords."[8] He who in God's own book wears these titles and is described as possessing these attributes, must be God. If the Father is God, the Son is God by the same marks of divinity.

The divinity of the Holy Spirit has been

[1] Matt. xxviii. 20. [2] John i. 13. [3] Heb. i. 3.
[4] John i. 4. [5] 1 Tim. i. 16. [6] Acts xvii. 31.
[7] Rev. i. 8. 1 Tim. 6. 15.

proved in a preceding chapter ; and thus it is clearly established that the Father, the Son, and the Holy Ghost are severally set before us in the New Testament under the name and with the attributes of God.

Are there then three Gods?—three distinct beings each of whom is a complete God? We hold fast the first truth established by the Scriptures — that there is only one living and true God. We cannot set that aside—we cannot modify it. The Bible does not contradict itself. There is but "one God and one Mediator between God and men ;" and to make other gods than one is sin.

Whatever is meant by ascribing the names and the attributes of God severally to the Father, and to the Son, and to the Holy Ghost, it cannot be meant that there are three Gods.

Is then the name of God applied to two of the three in some accommodated or restricted sense, and are the attributes deriv-

[1] 1 Tim. ii. 5.

ative and subordinate in the Son and in the Holy Ghost? But there is no indication of a qualified use of language, or of subordination in attributes, in the texts that ascribe to the Son and to the Holy Ghost the names and the powers of God. There is just as much propriety in limiting these when applied to the Father, as when given to the Son, or to the Holy Ghost. In each case the titles are absolute, the attributes complete, and we violate every rule of language if we attempt to qualify them. Beside—these three, Father, Son and Holy Ghost, are associated upon one parallel, or with an equal reverence and significance, in the solemn acts of baptism and of benediction; the covenant is with each and all alike; the blessing is from each and all alike.

Are, then, these three but different official or modal manifestations of God, different representations under which he appears to men, himself having the while but one proper personality? The Pope, for instance, is head of the Roman Catholic

Church throughout the world; he is the temporal sovereign of Rome, and he is a member of some particular order. Abraham Lincoln was a citizen of Illinois, the President of the United States, and the commander-in-chief of the army and navy. Now, does this idea of three several relations, three distinct modes of manifestation or action, fairly express the Biblical Trinity? By no means. For in every such case there is throughout but one person, having but one consciousness, in each and all these relations. Mr. Lincoln acted now in his civil character as President, and again in the military phase of that character, while as a citizen of Springfield he paid his town-taxes; but he, as President, did not speak to himself as commander, and say, "I, the President, send thee, the commander, to look after thy homestead, thou citizen of Springfield." This were absurd; for all the while there was but one and the same consciousness. But the peculiarity of the Biblical Trinity is that each of the three speaks *to* and *of* the others as distinct from himself; and each performs acts which the other does not. The Father sends the Son—the Son does not send the Father. The Son prays to the Father, the Father does not pray to the Son. The Son says, "I will pray the Father, and he shall give you another Comforter, even the Spirit of truth."[1] The Son returns to heaven in order that this other Comforter may come. The proofs of distinct personality, given in a preceding chapter, forbid the supposition that the names the Father, the Son, and the Holy Ghost denote merely different relations assumed by the same person. The Biblical Trinity is something more than a trinity of mode or manifestation.

From the teachings of the Scriptures we have the following induction of particulars concerning the Biblical doctrine of God:

(1.) There is one and only one God.

(2.) The Father, the Son, and the Holy

[1] John xiv. 16.

Ghost are set forth severally under the names and the attributes of God.

(3.) They are presented as distinct in acts and in consciousness.

(4.) They are made parallel in dignity and reality in the formula of baptism, and are there conjoined in one name.

The Facts the Basis of Faith.

THESE facts being all established by the Word of God, it remains to harmonize them in one proposition. But this is not necessary to receiving them as facts. Each of these four statements presents an intelligible fact, explicitly declared in the Scriptures. No philosophy of Being can demonstrate that there is any contradiction between these facts. It is therefore rational and scientific to receive them, each and all, upon the testimony of the Bible, though we may not be able to combine them into one philosophical proposition.

Moreover, it is reasonable to suppose and modest to admit, that there may be something in the nature of God which lies beyond our present comprehension; something concerning which he can instruct us by his word, and yet for which human language has no terms sufficiently clear and precise for the whole truth. We cannot affirm *a priori* that God exists or must exist thus and so; or that it is impossible he should exist in any manner different from our conception. We learn much concerning God from the constitution of our own minds; but God is not a man immensely magnified! We cannot find out the Almighty unto perfection. These Biblical statements concerning the divine existence can best be harmonized by some special adjustment of our ideas of *being* and of *person*. In common speech these are often confounded; but we know our personal identity only through consciousness; others know this only by its attributes; while of *being*, we know absolutely nothing. For what is spirit? What is the essence or substratum of the soul? We can only say that God is such a *Being* in his substance that he exists in a *three-fold personality* with respect to attributes and consciousness, without thereby dividing or qualifying the oneness of the substance. We believe in one God, the Father, and the Son, and the Holy Ghost.

CHAPTER XI.

THE TRINITY IN REDEMPTION.

Man's Need of the Father.

EACH person of the Trinity is revealed in a distinct relation to the work of man's redemption—the Father, the Son, and the Holy Ghost together making this the highest manifestation of the wisdom, the grace, the glory of God. Every soul that embraces the Gospel is a witness to the redemptive work of each person of the Godhead:—" elect according to the foreknowledge of God the Father, through sanctification of the Spirit, unto obedience and sprinkling of the blood of Jesus Christ."[1]

[1] 1 Peter i. 2.

There is a special adaptation to man's condition and wants in the Trinity as thus revealed. As a creature, weak and dependent, man needs the thoughtful love of the infinite Father. Though he has alienated his soul from God by sin, he can find no comfort in Atheism; since the thought that above this world of sin and wrong there is no God of truth and right, is more dreadful than the thought that a God of justice is on the throne—who, though we have offended him, is still the God of love. Man, needy and dependent, cannot find repose in the mere lap of nature—now soft with flowers and balmy wiith fragrance, and again hard, stern and frozen. Nature addresses the senses, the reason, the taste, the imagination, but nature cannot respond to the heart with the living warmth of love. Physical laws are fixed, and whether kind or severe in their bearing upon the individual, they are unchanging. Man may learn to adapt himself to them, but he cannot move them by his own emotions, nor feel emotion from them. There is no love nor pity in a law of nature.

The notion of a mysterious power or energy in the universe—whether we call it Fate, or Providence, or Divinity—affords man nothing to lean upon, to trust in, to love, so long as this remains an abstraction, without personality, without heart. There are painful perplexities in human affairs, private and public, personal, social, commercial, political, harrowing reverses often, in which man's wisdom and strength are as nothing, and for which there is no relief in metaphysical abstractions concerning the course of events, and the mysteries of life. Man needs one above himself to think for him, to plan for him, and above all, to love him.

Nature alone, would teach us the naked goodness and the naked justice of God—sometimes apparently irreconcilable in the course of human affairs—and one or the other of these conceptions predominates in the old Pagan theodicies and in monotheism, whether Jewish, Mohammedan, or rationalistic. Only through the revelation of the Trinity do we gain a conception of that love which shows mercy to the sinner, and yet in so doing maintains justice in the moral universe, and promotes holiness in the individual reclaimed. Here God is more than Sovereign, more than Lawgiver, more even than Father in the vague sense of paternity by creation; he has emotions, he has sympathies, he has moral affections, he has pardoning grace.

Man's Need of the Son.

BUT the sense of want and dependence is not the only feeling that troubles us; there is a feeling deeper and far more painful in the sense of sin; and, therefore, though we know that in his own nature God is a Father, and disposed to regard his creatures with paternal love, we may doubt whether he will be a Father to us, since we have offended Him by disobedience, by impurity, by wilfulness, by selfishness, by all manner of iniquity; and guilt demands atonement, satisfaction to justice which we are all inadequate to render, and guilt incurs penalty which we are unable to avert.

How wondrous here the adaptation of that revelation of God which brings him nigh as a Savior, and thus causes us to know him as a Father! What precious words are these—"if any man sin, we have an advocate with the Father, Jesus Christ the righteous;" and "the blood of Jesus Christ his Son cleanseth us from all sin."[1] This Sonship in the Godhead revealed as the Redeemer, is the wondrous adaptation of the Trinity to our need of reconciliation. "He that spared not his own Son, but delivered him up for us all, how shall he not with him also freely give us all things?"[2]

[1] John i. 7 and ii. 1. [2] Rom. viii. 32.

Man's Need of the Spirit.

BUT the soul thus redeemed from penalty, and brought to know God as a reconciled Father, feels at once the aspiration to become like God. The privilege of redemption, the consciousness of reconciliation, brings with it the longing for purity; a new life is stirred within the heart, a new purpose of living takes possession of the man; and freed from the bondage and curse of sin, he would fain be freed from its every trace and stain, in thought, imagination, habit, even in the members of the body once the willing agents and abettors of iniquity. But who is sufficient for these things? Who can lift himself out of his old earthliness, even when the shell is broken, and soar away toward God and heaven? Who that has tried this in his own strength, has not been baffled by the instability of his purpose, by the feebleness of his endeavors, by the power of some easily besetting sin? As in a vision, he had seen an angel of light beckoning him to the upper glory; he has seemed to follow with that exhilarating freedom with which the mind in dreams will vault out of the body into the regions of pure spirit; when suddenly some old habit of earth and sense seizing him as with the clamps of night-mare, drags him down, and he awakes with his own groaning to see the blissful vision vanish, and to bewail again, "Oh wretched man that I am, who shall deliver me from this body of death?"[1] But just here, in his utmost necessity, when all that Christ has done for him would else be lost, there comes to him a Spirit indeed; not a vision of the night, not a phantom of the imagination, but the Spirit of light, of truth, of holiness, who enters the heart and whispers, "Abba, Father," assuring it that the sanctification for which it struggles and yearns is the very will of God concerning it; and who Himself abides in the will-

[1] Rom. vii. 24.

ing, praying mind as in a temple, and sanctifies all its outgoings of thought, affection, purpose, will. He may become holy by this helping Spirit. And so the Trinity as related to man's redemption, instead of being a dry dogma of theology is a living power in the heart, bringing to all the conditions and necessities of man the loving Father the redeeming Son, the sanctifying Spirit.

The Trine-redemption the most glorious Manifestation of God.

THE work of man's redemption alone acquaints us with the glorious mystery of the divine existence in the persons of the Father, and the Son, and the Holy Ghost. Nothing in the material universe had ever revealed this mystery of the being of God, whereby he himself has society in unity, and whereby he adapts himself to all the wants of intelligent creatures. God is not an infinite solitude of Being—not a Mont

Blanc lifted above all other existence only to stand in cold, solitary, inaccessible grandeur. Though high above the heaven of heavens, he dwells in love—having within his own nature the social element of being which love demands ; and by this also communicating with his creatures, in modes and relations that bring him near and make him dear to every heart that is willing to know and enjoy him.

We may conceive of God in his simple unity of Being, as the Creator, the Governor, the Preserver of the world ;—but in Redemption the three persons whom the Scriptures reveal as existing in that unity, are all engaged, with varying offices and relations, but equal power, interest and glory.

They engage in it also with their direct activity as persons. The physical universe has its appointed laws, to which every orb and every atom is alike obedient; and the grandeur of their scope and the precision of their movement fill us with admiration and delight. The world of Providence, in the course of the seasons and the productions of the earth, has its appointed laws, and the regularity of their working, and the extent and variety of their combinations, are subjects for praise and thanksgiving. But in this personal agency of the triune God in Redemption, we behold a wonder and glory transcending all that Nature and Providence have revealed, by as much as the spiritual and eternal transcends the physical and the temporal. For, this work of man's redemption, begun in the counsels of the divine mind before the world was, sweeps through all the ages of time, from eternity unto eternity. It lay in the loving thought of God the Father before the foundation of the world; it was announced in the world as soon as the curse of sin had entered Eden; it was the central thought in the religion and the history of that people whom Jehovah called to be his own. Yet it was not left to words and signs and ordinances; God was in it still; and when the groaning ages cried for a Deliverer, and prophecy gave birth to expectation, then "in the fullness of time" the Son of God was manifest in the flesh, and suffered and died for our redemption. Nor was even the sublime truth of the incarnation left to do its own teaching in the world—the church, the ministry, the sacraments, the system of gospel truth and ordinances made the alone agencies for the furtherance of this work. But God is in it still;—the Holy Spirit—the third in the blessed unity of the Godhead, is in the world forevermore till redemption shall be fulfilled in the life everlasting. And his advent, we have seen, is the crowning wonder and glory of the work of redemption; for by the Holy Spirit, God comes nearer to us than when he talked with Abraham as a Father, nearer to us than when Jesus sat lovingly in the midst of his disciples, and bade them eat his flesh and drink his blood; for this coming of the Holy Ghost is no one visible phenomenon, no single memorable event to look back upon in history—but a presence, an abiding, in most intimate communication with the soul of man. It is a coming into the sphere of *mind*, of thought, feeling, affection, as distinguished from outward phenomena—and is in its own nature the highest manifestation of God to man.

Man ennobled by this Redemption.

WHAT an argument for the worth of the soul is given in this Trine-manifestation of God for its salvation;—the Father bending over it with a compassionate longing for its recovery; the Son dying for its redemption; the Spirit seeking, striving, pleading, that he may win it to holiness!

What a warrant for faith and hope in labors to bring men to God, is given in the fact that he who "spared not his own Son, but delivered him up for us all," has sent the Holy Spirit to prosecute the work of man's restoration by his personal presence and power. The renovation of the soul is not a scheme of humanitary philosophy, of socialistic reform. It is the purpose and work of God; it engages his whole being, and partakes of the greatness and the glory of his nature.

Through this Trine-manifestation man is raised to fellowship with God. Since the Word was made flesh and the Spirit has come into the world to abide, man may know God not only through contemplation, but by communion. Through Christ Jesus we have access by the Spirit unto the Father;[1] "our fellowship is with the Father and with his Son Jesus Christ;"[2] and it is given us to be "strengthened with might by the Spirit in the inner man" that we may "be filled with all the fullness of God."[3] No philosophy of human development, no philanthropic dream of progress can approach this redeeming, ennobling, sanctifying love of the Triune God. Though the

[1] Eph. ii. 18. [2] 1 John i. 3.
[3] Eph. iii. 19.

reason may not grasp it, the heart can take it in. We will lift up the gates of the soul, the everlasting doors of praise and joy, that this Redeeming King may enter in!

Glory be to the FATHER,
And to the SON,
And to the HOLY GHOST;

As it was in the beginning,
Is now, and ever shall be,
World without end. Amen.

www.ingramcontent.com/pod-product-compliance
Lightning Source LLC
LaVergne TN
LVHW011210110826
845150LV00006B/1387